From Budapest to the Korean War

Hungarian Physicians in North Korea, 1950–1957

From Budapest to the Korean War: Hungarian Physicians in North Korea, 1950-1957

This Edition was published by Jipmoondang in 2021, Seoul, Korea.

Jipmoondang
5th Floor, 82 Donhwamun-ro, Jongno-gu, Seoul, 03134, Korea
Phone: +82-1811-7567
E-mail: sale@jipmoon.com
Homepage: www.jipmoon.com

ISBN 978-89-303-1909-6 93900

Printed in Korea

From Budapest to the Korean War

Hungarian Physicians in North Korea, 1950–1957

Dr. Mózes Csoma
Ambassador of Hungary to Korea

JIPMOONDANG

Contents

PREFACE

The Korean War started out as a clash between the two rival Korean governments in Pyongyang and Seoul. However, it was not long before it evolved into a huge international conflict. As it is well known from the pages of the history books, five countries – Sweden, India, Denmark, Norway and Italy – provided medical support for South Korea. Meanwhile, some of the former Soviet bloc countries including Hungary, Romania, Bulgaria and Czechoslovakia, established hospitals in different provinces of North Korea. Hungary was the first among the Central and Eastern European states which sent its medical teams to the battlefield, and more than 200 Hungarian physicians, paramedics and nurses served there, divided into eight groups, arriving in the country consecutively between 1950 and 1957. At first, the institution was called 'Mátyás Rákosi Hospital' named after the general secretary of the Hungarian Working People's Party.[1)] However, after the purge of Rákosi by the Soviets in the summer of 1956, the institution was just referred to as the 'Hungarian Hospital in Korea'. Meanwhile, according to the North Korean documents, the institution was referred to as the 'Hospital No. 58 of the Korean People's Army'.

The mission of the Hungarian medical teams was unprecedented from various aspects. For example, it was the first

1) Rákosi, Mátyás (1892-1971): Hungarian communist. He served in the Austro-Hungarian army during the WW1 and was captured by the Tsarist Russian army. He became a communist in Soviet-Russia. After WW2, he became the *de facto* ruler of communist Hungary in his capacity as prime minister and general secretary of the party.

time that a relatively great number of Hungarian physicians left for the Far East to work there permanently. Furthermore, their destination was the most apocalyptic place on Earth at that time; it was quite difficult to keep in touch with their family members in Hungary, and the only way to communicate was through letters, which were forwarded by diplomatic couriers to the Hungarian legation in North Korea. However, communication with the Hungarian diplomats was often unsolvable, especially during the autumn of 1950.

More than 200 Hungarian physicians, paramedics and nurses served in a cultural environment they were totally unfamiliar with. They had chance to observe the Northern part of the Korean Peninsula in different phases of the war: during the summer of 1950, when Seoul had still belonged to North Korea, and during the evacuation in the autumn of 1950. Meanwhile, they were able to make some important observations about the Soviet Union, and particularly, about the situation in Manchuria, where the traces of the past Japanese rule were still noticeable at that time. It is interesting to mention that, despite the communist ideology, some minor elements of capitalism did exist both in the Soviet Union and in China. In the second year of the Korean War, the Hungarian hospital was relocated to Mangyongdae, which is famous for being the birthplace of Kim Il-sung. The hospital had temporarily operated in Huichon and Songrim too, but in the postwar years it was relocated to Sariwon city.

The Hungarian medical teams played a very important role in personal exchange between the two nations as well. During their time in the Far East, they formed deep friendships with North Koreans, and the first international marriages between the two nations were also recorded. However, due to the forming of close relationships, the Hungarians inevitably witnessed the internal turbulences in the North Korean regime, which targeted their official partners and good friends among others. To give an instance, the Korean director of the Hungarian hospital, Dr. Ri Kang-guk, was one of the victims of the political campaign against the communists who came from the Southern part of the Korean Peninsula.[2)] According to several recollections featuring that era, he was an open-minded and intelligent man who spoke fluent German. His deputy at the hospital was Major Hwang Su-bong, who was also a very talented man. According to a reminiscence, he exceled at organizing and managing, could play the piano and the flute, had good singing skills, was interested in poems and spoke German fluently.[3)] Another reminiscence emphasized that Major Hwang spoke very good English and French, too. However, Major Hwang Su-bong was also arrested only four month after the purge of the aforementioned director. His further fate remained unknown.

Apart from the lively personal exchange between the Hungarians and the Koreans, the eight groups of the medical teams played a significant role in the cultural interactions, too. As one of the outstandingly well-equipped medical institutions in North Korea, the Hungarian hospital treated leading Korean intellectuals and artists during and after the war. Among others, the following people were treated there: the forgotten Korean poet Seol Chung-sik who wrote an epos to the Hungarian physicians; the

---

2) Ri Kang-guk (1906-1955): Korean communist. He was born in Yangju in Kyonggi Province and studied at the Kyongseong Imperial University (today's Seoul National University). In 1932, he moved to Germany, where he studied at the Berlin University and joined to the communist movement. In 1935, he returned to Korea and continued his communist activities in Wonsan. In 1938, he was arrested by the colonial authorities. Right after the national liberation, he participated in the failed attempt to establish the People's Republic of Korea. In late 1946, he moved to the North, where he became secretary general of the North Korean People's Committee. After serving years in various posts of the regime, he was purged and sentenced to death during the campaign against the communists who came from the South.

3) Reminiscences of János Dénes (1943–1950–1958), 15. Archive of the Semmelweis Medical History Museum (Hungary, Budapest)

famous Korean actor Hwang Chul who lost his right hand during a bombardment; the communist intellectual Ahn Mak, the husband of the legendary dancer, Choi Seung-hee; and the famous Korean poet Yim Hwa who was interested in translating the poems of the most representative Hungarian poet to Korean. It can be seen as one of the characteristics of the communist regime that almost all of the aforementioned persons were purged sooner or later.

During its seven-year-long operation, the Hungarian hospital and its workers witnessed the changes in the relations between the Central and Eastern European countries and North Korea. At first, around the beginning of the Korean War, the Soviet bloc countries expressed their solidarity through various forms of support. However, from the beginning of the de-Stalinization and particularly after the Hungarian revolution against the Soviet rule in 1956, the bilateral relations became distant. When the last Hungarian medical team left North Korea in 1957, the members erected a bilingual monument to the memory of the Hungarian physicians, paramedics and nurses who served there. The monument, which the writer of this book visited officially in his capacity as the Ambassador of Hungary to Korea, can still be found in the garden of the 'People's Hospital of North Hwanghae Province' in Sariwon city.

Many people gave me help during the composition of this book. Therefore, I would like to express my gratitude particularly to the following persons: *Prof. Dr. József Padányi* (former vice rector of the University of Public Service, Budapest); *Dr. Péter Tálas* (institute director of the University of Public Service, Budapest); *Fanni Nagy-Lukács* (Photo Archive of the Hungarian Ministry of Defense, Budapest); *Dr. József Szabó* (Photo Archive of the Hungarian Ministry of Defense, Budapest); *Mr. Benedek Varga* (director of the Hungarian National Museum); *Dr. László Magyar* (vice director of the Semmelweis Medical History Museum, Budapest); *Dr. Katalin Szabó* (museologist at the Semmelweis

Medical History Museum, Budapest); *Dr. Janina Kulka* (daughter of pulmonologist Dr. Frigyes Kulka); *Dr. Mária Sátori* (daughter of physician Dr. Ödön Sátori); *Éva Ditrói* (daughter of otolaryngologist Dr. Sándor Ditrói); *Dr. Anna Székács* (professor of the Budapest Business School). I also thank to *Lee Jia*, *Luca Szabó* and *Bence Surányi* for their cooperation during the text's proofreading.

Finally, I would like to thank my wife, *Nam Sunmi* and my three sons, *János Chanu*, *Péter Seungu* and *István Jiu* for their continuous support. I particularly thank to *János Chanu* for his contribution in the digital correction of the archive photos.

Seoul, January 2021
The author

I. Historical background and antecedents

Geographically, Hungary and the Korean Peninsula are located very far from each other, but the two nations have common historical roots somewhere in Asia, which was testified by the ural-altaic family of the Hungarian and Korean language. The *magyar* tribes had wandered to Europe for several centuries and arrived in the Carpathian basin in the late 9th century A.D. The first-ever Hungarian state was established by I. (Saint) Stephen in the year of 1000 when the Georyo kingdom started its fights with the khitans. The Hungarians recognized the Roman catholicism as their state religion and continued to retain the feudal state. The country was attacked by the Mongols in 1241, ten years after the outbreak of the war between the Great Mongolian Empire and Georyo. We can observe more parallelism between the Hungarian and the Korean history: both nations reached the peak of their feudal culture in the 15th century. The Hungarian king I. Matthias (r. 1458-1490) was famous for his royal library (Bibliotheca Corviniana) which was an outstanding cultural creation at that time. Therefore, the character of I. Matthias is comparable to king Sejong the Great (r. 1418-1450); who had ordered the creation of the Korean national writing system. In the following centuries, the Hungarians fought against the foreign intrusion several times, particularly against the Ottoman Empire in the 15th and 16th century and against the Habsburg Empire in the 18th and 19th century. However, when the the Korean seaports started to open in the second half of the 19th century, the Hungarians had already reconciled with the Austrians and lived together in the form of a dual monarchy called Austro-Hungarian Empire. In that time, the first Hungarians arrived to the Korean Peninsula; two among the gentlemen were physicians who managed to treat some Korean patient for a short time. We can say that it was the antecedent of the Hungarian medical support to North Korea in the 1950's.

The first visit of Hungarians to the Korean Peninsula was in 1890. When the Austro-Hungarian steam corvette 'Zrínyi' arrived at the port of Chemulpho to establish diplomatic relations with the 'Hermit Kingdom', the Korean officials did not allow any kinds of diplomatic negotiations as it was the national mourning period. However, the real reason was probably other than the Queen Shinjeong's death. The Austro-Hungarians were escorted in Seoul by the German consul who was a resident in the Korean capital, but this led some Korean officials to thinking that Austro-Hungary was a vassal state of Germany.[1] Even though the establishement of the diplomatic relations was postponed but signed only two years later, what the vessel's phycians observed during the mission on the corvette 'Zrínyi' is a great historical significance.

The medical doctor on board was Dr. Ferenc Gáspár (1861-1923) who wrote a detailed reminiscence about his journey to East Asia. His relationship with Korea first started in Nanking when he was on the way to the Far East. He and his fellows were invited to the residence of a Chinese nobleman where they had an opportunity to taste 'Corean style' pork meat.[2] Arriving at the

---

1) Park Song-sun, "Hanguk tongripundongkwa Honggari" (The Korean independence movement and Hungary – in Korean) *Hangukkwa Honggari tongripundongui kiokkwa kyocha.* (The memories of the Korean and the Hungarian independence movements – in Korean) Jukjeon: Dankook University, 2019, 119.

2) Gáspár, Ferenc: *Vitorlával Ázsia körül.* (With sails around Asia – in Hungarian) Budapest: Singer és Wolfner, 1907, 392.

Dr. Ferenc Gáspár, the Hungarian navy physician who visited the Chosun Kingdom in 1890
(From the collection of the author)

coasts of the 'Hermit Kingdom', the Hungarian physician observed the legacy of the long isolation: in the estuary of the rivers were dikes built to prevent the foreign ships from entering the country.[3] In Chemulpo, Dr. Gáspár met with Pater Wilhelm, a German missionary who had been living in Korea for a long time and helping the local residents as a paramedic. The missionary asked the Hungarian physician to join him to treat the patients in the neighboring villages. Dr. Gáspár found the local villages very poor. The houses in the villages were made of mud and straw. The small houses sometimes accommodated 8 to 10 people usually with poor hygiene. According to his reminiscence, he sometimes felt nausea due to the poor condition of the houses and left the place immediately. Years later, a Hungarian folklorist strongly criticized Dr. Gáspár for his narrow observations which were limited to the surroundings of the port of Chemulpo and his over-generalization on the circumstances of the Korean Peninsula.[4] Nevertheless, the

3) Gáspár, *Vitorlával Ázsia körül*, 424.

4) Baráthosi, Balogh Benedek: *Korea, a hajnalpír országa.* (Korea, land of the morning calm – in Hungarian) Budapest: A szerző kiadása, 1929, 3.

reminiscences of Dr. Gáspár are obviously important because these were the first observations made by a Hungarian in the Far Eastern country.

The second Hungarian medical doctor visited the Korean Peninsula in 1908 when the country was already a Japanese protectorate. Dr. Dezső Bozóky (1871−1957) served on the cruiser 'Kaiser Franz Josef I.', a flagship of the Austro-Hungarian Empire in East Asia. The warship passed the sea route between China and Japan several times, but due to the unstable situation in Korea – dethronement of the Emperor Gojong and the resistance of the former Korean army –, the captain of the ship decided to postpone the visit to Korea. Finally, in 1908, the ship arrived at the port of Chemulpo where Dr. Bozóky saw large construction work being processed to reduce the impact of the ebb and flow of the tide.[5] The visitor described Chemulpo in his book as a modern city: the physician saw the European-style buildings of the Japanese marine companies and banks, the red postboxes which he had already seen in Japan and the wires of the telegraph equipment everywhere.[6] At that time, Chemulpo and Seoul were already connected by a railroad which enabled the Austro-Hungarians to reach the Korean capital by train. After spending only one day in Seoul, the cruiser 'Kaiser Franz Josef I.' moved Southward to the island of Port Hamilton (Komun-do), on which a British naval base had been operated two decades earlier. When Dr. Bozóky and his fellows visited the island, they did not see any sign of the former British presence while they witnessed the presence of the Japanese who had installed a telegraph antenna on the highest point of the island. Small Korean rafts approached the Austro-Hungarian warship and

---

5) Bozóky, Dezső: *Két év Keletázsiában. China és Korea.* (Two years in East Asia. China and Korea – in Hungarian) Nagyvárad: A szerző kiadása, 1911, 490.

6) Bozóky, *Két év Keletázsiában*, 488.

Dr. Dezső Bozóky, the Hungarian navy physician who visited the Korean Empire in 1908
(From the collection of the author)

some naked Korean kids offered fish and shells to the servicemen on board to exchange them for clothes. Soon after, Korean adults also showed up to receive medical treatement from the doctor on the cruiser. Dr. Bozóky worried about the possibility of encountering exotic diseases the aboriginals might carry. Therefore, he went down to a small vessel to take care of the local patients. According to his reminiscence, he found that the local charlatans treated the wound and ulcer of the patients with steer manure and tiger hair. The doctor had to get rid of the diseased part completely.[7)]

Dr. Dezső Bozóky observed the last moment of the Korean Empire with his own eyes. He witnessed the modernization and the transformation of the country which was initiated by the Japanese, which is sad and positive at the same time: the old Korea had gone forever, but the living standard of the locals was about to improve. He concluded that it was a better option for Korea to be ruled by the Japanese than by the 'Russian bear'. What the physician had experienced during the visit to Vladivostok obviously led him to the conclusion.[8] When the first group of the Hungarian medical teams left for North Korea in the summer of 1950, the former navy physician, Dr. Bozóky, was 69 years old. It is a very interesting, yet-to-be-answered question whether any of the younger doctors who were going to head for Korea ever contacted Dr. Bozóky to ask him to share his experiences in the East Asian countries.

7) Bozóky, *Két év Keletázsiában*, 521-526.

8) Bozóky, *Két év Keletázsiában*, 487-488.

II. The first group to Korea. Establishing the hospital in Chunghwa

At dawn on June 25, 1950, the Korean People's Army (KPA) launched a surprise attack against South Korea. In the countries of the Soviet tomb, the mass media announced the declaration of the DPRK' Ministry of Internal Affaires, which claimed that the South Korean troops attacked first, but the KPA forces 'repelled the offensive'. The develpoments on the divided peninsula created a huge solidarity movement for North Korea in the Soviet tomb. In Hungary, the solidarity campaign was coordinated by the Hungarian Peace Council and the Democratic Association of Hungarian Women. Their first mass event was held in Budapest on July 15, 1950, which announced the sending of a field hospital to Korea. To cover the costs of the hospital, a nationwide fundraising movement was launched in Hungary, which yielded more than 5 million Hungarian forints. At that time, the average monthly salary was around 1,000 forints. It is interesting to mention that the aforementioned mass event which was held in Budapest is introduced in the North Korean novel *50nyon yeoreum* (Summer '50). The book describes the first months of the Korean War from a North Korean point of view and particularly mentions the solidarity rally in Budapest.[1)]

On July 20, 1950, the Hungarian medical team boarded a

---

1) Ahn Dong-chun: *50nyon yeoreum*. (Summer '50 – in Korean) Pyongyang: Munhwa Yaesul Jonghap Chulphansa, 2001, 316-317.

The departure of the first group of the Hungarian medical teams from the Ferihegy Airport of Budapest on July 20, 1950
(Semmelweis Medical History Museum, Budapest)

Soviet-made Li-2 aircraft in the newly built Budapest Ferihegy International Airport and after a two hour flight, landed in Moscow. There, as written in the reminiscences of a female paramedic, Karádi, they were welcomed by the Hungarian and the North Korean diplomats.[2)] The physicians were accommodated in Hotel National, where they spent three nights. After visiting the local tourist attractions, including the Moscow subway, they were invited for a dinner to the North Korean embassy. However, the Korean dishes did not match some of the Hungarians' taste. On July 24, the team departed from Moscow and continued their journey to East Asia via Kazan, Omsk, Novosibirsk and Irkutsk, where they were vaccinated against cholera. Since Soviet planes flew only during daylight hours at that time, all of the travelers spent the nights at the hotels of the local airports. The medical team arrived in Mukden

2) Karády, Györgyné: *Magyar sebész orvos-egészségügyiek első koreai csoportjának menekülése az amerikai hadsereg elől Kínába.* (The escape of the first Hungarian medical team to China frontwards the American troops – manuscript in Hungarian), 1. Archive of the Semmelweis Medical History Museum (Hungary, Budapest)

Hungarian doctors are waving when boarding the Li-2 plane of the Soviet Aeroflot airline
(Semmelweis Medical History Museum, Budapest)

(today's Shenyang), Northeast China on July 26, where the weather was hot and humid. The Hungarians experienced culture shock for various reasons. For example, it was their first time to see Chinese style houses and rickshaws, dirty streets with thousands of flies buzzing around and children with poor hygiene hanging out. Also, in the evening, during a reception, the physicians had the opportunity to have their first encounter with Chinese gastronomy. According to the recollections of Karádi, crab, mussel and octopus were served, which were quite unfamiliar and unusual for them. Furthermore, the chicken seemed to have been prepared with sugar. As for the drinks, the paramedic mentions the Korean word 'saida', which refers to any carbonated beverages. Although the word 'saida' is based on the English word 'cider', it was the Japanese transcription of the original word that was adopted into Korean.[3)]

The Hungarians took a train and left Mukden for the Chinese border city of Andong (today's Dandong), where they arrived on July 27, 1950. At the railway station, the Hungarians experienced culture shock again. They saw half-naked men stroll along the narrow streets crowded with vendors. Due to the hot temperature, locals used hand fans and wet towels, and the Hungarians followed their habit. According to Karádi, Hungarian men were much faster to adopt to the new circumstances than women, so soon after their arrival, they organized a table tennis match wearing wet towels on their heads. After spending two days in Andong, the Hungarians got in trucks and crossed the Amnok (Yalu) River overnight. At that time, the bridge on the river was still intact.

The Hungarian medical team – including seven surgeons, five operating theatre assistants, one internist and one political leader – arrived to North Korea on July 28, 1950. Since it was dangerous to travel in the daytime, they stopped in villages, covered the trucks with tree branches for camouflage and only hit the mountainous roads after the sun set. The physicians usually spent their days at streambanks near the villages. It took two days for them to travel from the border to Pyongyang, and they noticed that the villages and

---

3) Karády, *Magyar sebész...*, 1.

The building of the Hungarian legation in Pyongyang in July 1950
(National Archives of Hungary, Ministry of Foreign Affairs' Directory)

bridges were guarded by soldiers; this was also mentioned by a Hungarian doctor in an interview given to the Korean Central News Agency.[4] The first impressions about North Korea were good. Karádi spoke highly of Koreans, emphasizing their kindness, modesty and especially their cleanliness, which was in sharp contrast with what she had previously experienced in China.[5]

On the morning of July 29, 1950, the North Korean Ministry of Foreign Affairs contacted the Hungarian legation in Pyongyang and informed them that the physicians would arrive around 10 o'clock on the same day and that they would be welcomed in a village 20-25 kilometers away from the capital.[6] The Hungarian envoy, Sándor Simics, and the legation's first secretary, Mária Balog

---

4) Report written on August 16, 1950, by the Hungarian envoy Sándor Simics. MNL XIX-J-14 box no. 1. National Archives of Hungary, Ministry of Foreign Affairs' Directory (Hungary, Budapest)

5) Karády, *Magyar sebész...*, 2.

6) Report written on August 16, 1950, by the Hungarian envoy Sándor Simics. MNL XIX-J-14 box no. 1.

intended to go to the venue directly by the legation's car, escorted by an official from the Protocol Department of the Foreign Ministry. However, on their way there, they had to make a stop in front of the local police station because of an air raid on the village. The official stayed at the police station, and the two diplomats were sent to the neighboring hillside, where they waited for an hour and a half. However, the Hungarian medical team was nowhere to be found. Therefore the diplomats moved to the neighboring village where the evacuated staff of the Chinese Embassy were staying. The Chinese diplomats had a telephone in their building, so the Hungarians tried to call the Foreign Ministry several times from there, but they were given no information about the physicians. Around 5 o'clock in the afternoon, the diplomats headed back to Pyongyang where they met the representatives of the Ministry of Health of North Korea who were about to depart for the abovementioned village to pick up the Hungarian medical team. It was quite probable that the Health Ministry officials were much more informed about their exact arrival time than the Foreign Ministry. At 7 o'clock, Sándor Simics was called from the Foreign Ministry and was told that the physicians had arrived at the village, and they would arrive at the Intourist Hotel in Pyongyang by 8 o'clock. The envoy and the staff of the legation left to the hotel immediately, but both the medical team and the North Koreans were late. The protocol chief of the Foreign Ministry and the deputy minister of the Ministry of Health appeared at the venue at 9 o'clock, and finally, the Hungarians arrived at 11 o'clock. After politely exchanging greetings, the high-ranking Korean participants left, but the envoy and his staff stayed there until the physicians finished their late dinner.[7)]

As for the facilities of the Intourist Hotel, Karádi noticed

---

7) Report written on August 16, 1950, by the Hungarian envoy Sándor Simics. MNL XIX-J-14 box no. 1.

that the beds were equipped with mosquito nets, and there were only squatting toilets available. Also, there was no space that could be used as shelter in the building. During their first night, an air raid on the city interrupted the Hungarians' rest. They had to go down to the basement where the air was hot and sultry. Due to the lack of oxygen, one of the Korean helpers of the Hungarians collapsed in the basement, and it was Karádi who helped him gain consciousness, using a wet towel.[8] On the following morning, July 30, 1950, the medical team visited the Hungarian legation, but on the way there, another air raid began. Because of the unpleasant conditions in the Intourist Hotel, the diplomats decided to offer a temporary accommodation to the physicians at the legation.[9] According to the reminiscences of the female parademic, the city of Pyongyang was still almost totally unaffected by the war. She wrote that the vast majority of the buildings were made of wood and that it was hard to find any stone buildings there.[10]

In the evening of the same day, the medical team and the Hungarian diplomats were invited for a banquet dinner hosted by foreign minister Park Hon-yong and some other North Korean officials in the government's building. According to a report written by Sándor Simics, the event was no different from a usual one, but it turned out to be a bizarre experience in the end. The hosts and the guests were sitting around a huge table, and two young Korean staff members started to serve chocolates, candies and compotes. Later, the young ladies brought boiled eggs, sliced salami and Russian canned sweet peppers without any bread, and they also did not prepare any plates. The guests started to eat without plates, and Sándor Simics and Park ended up eating together from the same

---

8) Karády, *Magyar sebész…*, 3.

9) Report written on August 16, 1950, by the Hungarian envoy Sándor Simics. MNL XIX-J-14 box no. 1.

10) Karády, *Magyar sebész…*, 3.

Preparing for the arrival of the Hungarian physicians in the town of Chunghwa. The boughs on the roof were used for camouflaging the building
(National Archives of Hungary, Ministry of Foreign Affairs' Directory)

salver. After that, the girls served sliced watermelons and finally, brought some bread. At the end of the bizarre banquet, the plates arrived, too. The envoy wrote in his report that probably all of the food had previously been prepared in the kitchen, but the young ladies might have served it in the wrong order.[11)]

On the following morning, July 31, 1950, the Hungarian envoy and four physicians travelled to the city of Chunghwa, located about 25 kilometers south of the capital where they inspected the empty school building which was the designated place of the Hungarian hospital. The Hungarians were escorted by the deputy minister of the Ministry of Health of North Korea and by the chief physician of the Korean People's Army. The building was in a fairly good state although there was neither electricity nor running water.

---

11) Report written on August 16, 1950, by the Hungarian envoy Sándor Simics. MNL XIX-J-14 box no. 1.

The former school building in Chunghwa in which the Hungarian hospital was operated. The net on the wall was used for camouflage
(National Archives of Hungary, Ministry of Foreign Affairs' Directory)

Finally, the Hungarian medical team moved to the new location by bus, departing at 5 o'clock in the morning of August 2, with two trucks loaded with their belongings following them. Although the rooms were not repainted, the former school building was basically ready to function as a hospital. According to Karádi, the hospital got equipped in quite a short time. Electricity was produced by a gasoline generator, and water was regularly delivered with a tanker truck.[12] The new institution was able to accommodate approximately 500 patients, and the first 250 slightly injured people arrived on August 10. Nevertheless, a high-ranking cadre from the Ministry of Health of North Korea suggested that, since the hospital had skilled medical staff, they should receive severely injured patients only. On August 16, Sándor Simics visited the hospital and wrote in his report that the number of the patients increased to 460. While he

12) Karády, *Magyar sebész*..., 3.

The Hungarian physicians in the town of Chunghwa
(Semmelweis Medical History Museum, Budapest)

was there, an unofficial delegation from the neighboring village payed a visit to the hospital. The delegation consisted of local teachers, female and youth association representatives. They expressed their gratitude to the foreign physicians and gave them three boxes of locally produced apples. The physicians found the spontaneous visit really touching.[13] Sándor Simics reported to Budapest that the legation tried its best to help the medical team in every way possible; they forwarded the letters and telegrams to the physicians and also sent books and papers from the library of the legation to them. However, in the second half of August 1950, due to the continuous bombardments targeting the bridge on the Taedong River, the Hungarian legation and the hospital faced several difficulties regarding communication. As expected, telephone connection was not an available option at that time.[14]

---

13) Report written on August 16, 1950, by the Hungarian envoy Sándor Simics. MNL XIX-J-14 box no. 1.

14) Report written on August 31, 1950, by the Hungarian envoy Sándor Simics. MNL XIX-J-14 box no. 1.

Group photo of the Hungarian physicians in the town of Chunghwa
(Semmelweis Medical History Museum, Budapest)

Since it was located between two potential targets - a railway station and a tunnel -, the bombardments unavoidably affected the Hungarian hospital as well. Karádi wrote in her recollections that trenches were dug into the ground, where the staff and the patients could wait out the air raids. Because of the continuous danger, the patients preferred to constantly stay in the trench. According to Karádi, the Hungarians placed a huge red cross in the garden to warn the aircrafts that a hospital was located there. On August 29, 1950, at dawn, six aircrafts bombarded the hospital in Chunghwa, and one of the bombs hit and destroyed some of the small traditional Korean houses 20-30 meters away from the main building. The Hungarians were deeply shocked; a Korean physician and three Korean volunteer nurses who were staying in one of the small houses lost their lives. On the same day, the North Korean defense minister, Choi Yong-gon, sent a letter from Pyongyang to the director of the Hungarian hospital, in which he expressed his sadness about what happened.[15] Because of the

15) Letter written on August 29, 1950, by the North Korean defense minister

bombardment, on August 31, the Hungarian envoy and the legation's first secretary, Mária Balog, visited the hospital late in the evening. The diplomats reported to Budapest that the physicians did not panic.[16] Four days after the bombardment, the leading Hungarian daily paper *Szabad Nép* published that 'a hospital' was bombed in North Korea, but it did not say a single word about the fact that the destroyed hospital was the workplace of the Hungarian medical team. This shows the typical attitude of the media of that era.[17]

Choi Yong-gon. MNL XIX-J-14 box no. 1.

16) Report written on August 31, 1950, by the Hungarian envoy Sándor Simics. MNL XIX-J-14 box no. 1.

17) "Pak Hen En elvtárs, koreai külügyminiszter tiltakozása az ENSZ-nél" (Korean Minister of Foreign Affairs Comrade Park Hon-yong protests against the UN – in Hungarian) *Szabad Nép*, September 2, 1950.

III. Moving to Yangdok. Evacuation to Manchuria

In the early morning on September 4, 1950, the Hungarian hospital was again taken under continuous attacks. One of the patients, an injured North Korean air force officer, explained to the Hungarians during an air raid that the huge B-29 Superfortress bombers did not mean any danger to the hospital because their target was Pyongyang. However, the fighter jets which escorted the bombers flew at a very low altitude and often attacked the hospital and its neighborhood. According to Karádi, the fighters flown so low that even the helmets of the pilots were visible from the ground. Karádi emphasized in her recollections that the stay in Chunghwa was unbearable not only because of the bombardments but also because of the lack of running water. The Hungarian medical team and their local staff tried their best despite the rough circumstances; the small amount of water delivered with tanker trucks was boiled before use and the primitive toilets were disinfected with calcium hypochlorite as often as possible. Furthermore, in order to prevent the spread of contagious diseases, the patients were vaccinated against cholera and typhus.

One of the Hungarian physicians, Dr. Remete who also served as the party secretary of the medical team, wrote a letter about the circumstances in North Korea, and it was later published in the Hungarian daily *Szabad Nép*. The propagandistic letter introduced the hospital to the Hungarian readers, giving a detailed description about the institution's four departments, the head of each department being a Hungarian doctor and their deputies being Korean physicians. The Korean nurses were soldiers, and although most of them had never worked in a hospital before, they were very quick to adapt. Dr. Remete also described how the bombardments destroyed the wooden houses and how the locals were trying to survive the carpet-bombings in the trenches along the roads. However, he never mentioned the fact that the Hungarian hospital was also bombed continuously.[1] On September 8, 1950, when the tunnel of the neighboring hill was destroyed in a bombardment, dozens of the injured were taken to the hospital. Due to the continuous bombardments, the North Korean authorities decided to transfer the Hungarian medical team to Yangdok, 120 kilometers north of the capital. The Hungarians were told that since there are neither highways nor tunnels, the new place would be safe from the bombardments. Two days later, on September 10, the chief physician and the political leader of the Hungarian team left to Yangdok to inspect the new location. In the meantime, the physicians and the medical staff in Chunghwa started to pack their belongings. Finally, on September 12, at the crack of dawn, the medical team departed for Yangdok by four camouflaged trucks. Karádi left Chunghwa in the evening that day, and according to her recollections, they were worried about crossing the bombarded Pyongyang. The bridge over the Taedong River was already destroyed, and the only available option for crossing was a narrow pontoon bridge with a 3-kilometer-long line of cars waiting to pass over. At that time, the roads were bombarded by the aircrafts day and night. Karádi was in one of the trucks with seven North Korean soldiers, and after passing Pyongyang safely, the trucks turned on their headlamps. However, the town which had been believed to be safe

---

1) Remete, Tibor: "Magyar levél Koreából" (Hungarian letter from Korea – in Hungarian) *Szabad Nép*, September 24, 1950.

from the bombardments had already been destroyed by the time the trucks arrived.[2)]

The new hospital was set up in one of the sanatoriums of the Ministry of Interior of North Korea, 3 kilometers away from the town. Its operation theater and X-ray room were well-equipped, attracting a great number of patients. Furthermore, the Hungarians were deeply touched because even many of their former patients from Chunghwa followed them to the new location. However, according to the diplomatic report written by the Hungarian legation in North Korea, at first, the cooperation between the Hungarian team and the local cadre physicians was not quite free of troubles.[3)] Karádi mentioned in her recollections that the hospital

Györgyné Karádi, Hungarian paramedic
(Semmelweis Medical History Museum, Budapest)

2) Karády, *Magyar sebész*..., 5.

3) Diplomatic report prepared by the Hungarian legation in North Korea on December 31, 1950. MNL XIX-J-14 box no. 1. 1-59.

A destroyed truck somewhere in North Korea. The photo was taken by a member of the Hungarian medical team probably during the evacuation
(Semmelweis Medical History Museum, Budapest)

buildings had huge chimneys which made the location similar to an industrial plant. It was probably one of the reasons why the bombardments reached the region despite it being quite isolated, and the Hungarians soon had to face the same difficulties as they had experienced in Chunghwa. The medical supplies started to run out, and rumors stating that the truck which was to deliver food to the hospital was destroyed on its way there began to spread. Meanwhile, news emerged of the Americans reoccupying Seoul and moving forward to the north. According to Karádi, the Hungarians were worried that the American advance party would block the way to Shinuiju, which was believed to be one of the possible directions in case of evacuation.[4)]

Eventually, the Hungarian medical team left Yangdok on

4) Karády, *Magyar sebész*..., 6.

October 10, 1950. They headed to the direction of Manpho city on the northern border. However, it is hard to reconstruct the exact route of their evacuation from the archive sources which are available about their odyssey.[5] The team spent a day in a Korean peasant house, a few kilometers away from a mining town. Meanwhile, the whole region was under continuous bombardment. The local peasants were kind to the Hungarians and offered them various Korean dishes that the physicians found delicious. However, according to Karádi, the team suffered from the lack of bathroom, and some of them even got lice. On October 11 and 12, the medical team, heading northwest, continued its odyssey, covering 80 kilometers on terrible roads. The Hungarians passed the city of Huichon which was completely destroyed with only some chimneys visible over the ruins. Reaching the outskirts of the city, the Hungarians tried to cross the Chongchon River.[6] However, there was no bridge, and their truck got stuck in the middle of the river. The physicians left the vehicle and continued their way on foot in the thigh-high water. The women of the team were carried by the men. The next morning, the aforementioned Korean deputy director of the hospital, Major Hwang Su-bong and another officer, Captain Moon Ho, went back to the destroyed Huichon to call assistance to pull the truck out of the river. Finally, the problem was solved by some KPA soldiers, and the Hungarians gave them a big box of chocolate to thank them for their cooperation. According to Karádi, starvation was a serious problem in the North Korean army at that time.[7]

In the evening of October 12, 1950, the abovementioned

---

5) Diary of Ottó Diner (June 20, 1950 – July 19, 1951). Archive of the Semmelweis Medical History Museum (Hungary, Budapest)

6) Its ancient name was Salsu River which had been the place of the great medieval battle between the Goguryeo Kingdom (B.C. 37–668) and the Sui Empire (A.D. 581–618). This fact can be found on the history books.

7) Karády, *Magyar sebész…*, 8.

KPA officer, Captain Moon Ho, obtained a can of gasoline for the truck, and the Hungarian medical team continued their journey. Just when they were leaving the region of Huichon, the air raid started again. The physicians and the staff jumped off the truck and waited until the aircrafts passed. During that night, the Hungarians reached a town in the mountains from where the sounds of the American cannons were audible. The frontline was located approximately 40-50 kilometers away from that place. On October 13, the physicians reached the town of Chongchon where the local secretary of the Korean Worker's Party helped to accommodate the team in a traditional Korean house which was equipped with *ondol* heating system. In the case of those buildings, the kitchen was installed at the side of the house, and the smoke flowed through pipes under the floor of the rooms in order to generate heat inside. The tired physicians really enjoyed the sleep on the hot floor. However, Major Hwang and Captain Moon Ho obtained gasoline again, and they had to continue their evacuation. The trucks ran about 100 kilometers in the mountains. Karádi wrote that she was mortally afraid on the serpentine roads which were in extremely bad condition and did not have guard rails, either. Despite being on the road all night long, they were unable to reach their next stop, the city of Kanggye, before sunrise. They had to wait in a wooden house situated in the dreary mountains, but they soon moved to the nearby forest to avoid yet another air raid. In the evening, the staff removed the camouflage from the truck and checked whether if that the engine and the break system were damaged by the bullets or not. They have advanced approximately 60 kilometers with the headlamps on when a large crowd of people appeared along the road, shouting, waving and warning them to turn off the headlamps due to the air raid. They were locals from Kanggye who left the city because of the continuous bombardments. The Hungarians and the local citizens saw a flash and heard a big explosion from the direction of Kanggye, and for first time during their journey, the Hungarians heard the sound of anti-aircraft guns. Karádi mentioned in her recollections that the Koreans who saw the fate of their hometown, just repeated the same word: 'aygo, aygo'. In the night, the medical team crossed the burning city where the residents were collecting the injured and dead people from the ruins. During the sunrise in the dawn of October 15, the Hungarians beheld their final destination on the horizon, the city of Manpho near to the Chinese border.[8)]

Due to the sunrise, the medical team couldn't enter Manpho. Before completing the last 17 kilometers, they were waiting on the mountains from where they could also observe the unceasing fire around Kanggye. The Hungarians were informed by the North Koreans that the local authorities in Manpho were waiting for them, having their accommodation arranged with food and bathrooms provided. Examining the archive sources, it seems that since it was hard to find a safe route to Manpho, the Hungarians departed for the city only on the evening of October 16. On their way it was raining, and their truck rolled over on the slippery road. The physicians and the staff had to wait on the side of the road until some local residents helped them to pull the vehicle out of the ditch at dawn. Arriving at the city where the buildings were surprisingly intact despite the bombardments due to the relatively great number of anti-aircraft guns installed, the medical team was accommodated in the building of the local police regardless of the promise about the housing with bathroom. Later, they were taken to a traditional Korean house, and they started to work at the local hospital where there were only a few patients. The North Korean staff from the hospital of Yangdok soon arrived at Manpho to join the team, and some of the former patients came to seek treatment in the new

8) Karády, *Magyar sebész…*, 9-10.

hospital. On October 20, the Hungarian envoy, Sándor Simics who was also in North Korea at that time sent a telegram to the physicians to inform them that there were negotiations going on about their new location, but they would have to stay in Manpho until further notice. Two days later, on October 22, the medical team was visited by the North Korean health minister who discussed the team's possible relocation to the city of Andong (today's Dandong) from where the physicians had left China for North Korea in summer. However, due to its political significance, the final decision was that the Hungarian team had to stay in Korea.[9]

Karádi wrote in her recollections that the Chinese side of the border was heavily attacked by aircrafts on October 24. The following day, a great number of Chinese soldiers crossed the bridge over the Amnok (Yalu) River, heading to the direction of Manpho. On October 26, crowds of people arrived in Manpho from Manchuria by cars. As the Hungarians learned from Major Hwang, they were the whole personnel of the government of the DPRK. However, the next day at dawn, the medical team was suddenly ordered to immediately evacuate to Manchuria. The Hungarians panicked because they thought that the frontline had collapsed and their current location would soon become a battlefield. The bridge to Manchuria was just opened during the night. Therefore, many people were on their way to the border. Finally, the Hungarians arrived in the town of Jian in Jilin province on October 27 at 7:45 in the morning.[10] It is interesting to mention that the location of Jian played an important role in Korean history as the capital of the Koguryo Kingdom between the 1st and 5th century. The ruins of Kuknaesong, in particular, the *Memorial stele of King Kwanggaeto* and the *Tomb of the General* (Janggunchong) were rediscovered at

---

9) Diary of Ottó Diner.

10) Karády, *Magyar sebész...*, 11.

that time. However, the physicians certainly did not have the opportunity to observe the cultural relics regarding that there was a possibility that the WWIII might break out in the near future.

IV. From Jian to Changchun

The Hungarian medical team was accommodated in a Chinese barrack in Jian. However, there was no heating despite the cold weather. Meanwhile, hundreds of refugees from North Korea were wandering on the streets without housing, warm clothes or food. Karádi mentioned that she recognized a familiar face among the refugees: the local party secretary in Chunghwa, the first location of the Hungarian hospital. The party official said that he was ordered to go back to the occupied part of the country. In order to reach their destination, he and his fellows built a raft and rafted down the fast-running river. However, when an American paratrooper unit started to fire on the raft, most of his fellows died. He was able to survive because he jumped into the water and waited under the raft until it was safe to swim up to the surface.[1)]

The Hungarians were informed that the barrack they stayed in could become a possible military target. Therefore, they had no choice but to leave it. At that time, the fear from an American-Chinese clash, furthermore, from the WWIII was not irrational at all. It is necessary to emphasize that the Chinese Civil War between the Communists and the Kuomintang troops had ended only 1 year earlier, and the tension was still palpable in the Taiwan Strait. So the leadership of the Soviet Union strongly believed that the WWIII would broke out soon. Turning back to the Hungarians, the medical team waited for the guidance of the Hungarian envoy, Sándor

1) Karády, *Magyar sebész…*, 12.

Simics, but he wasn't available at that time. The physicians received contradictious information about him; one of the sources stated that the envoy had left Pyongyang together with the local diplomatic corps and he was already in Chinese territory, but according to another source, the envoy was said to be staying with the whole personnel of the North Korean government in Manpho. Hoping that the second source was right, the political leader and the chief physician of the Hungarian team alongside with Captain Moon Ho went back to Manpho on October 30 to find the Hungarian diplomats.[2)]

However, it was the first source that was closer to the truth: Sándor Simics and his staff were somewhere in North Korea, probably around the town of Shinuiju, together with other diplomats.[3)] According to the Hungarian diplomatic reports on November 1, the local post office refused to take over the diplomats' telegram messages. Shortly after that incident, the deputy minister from the North Korean Ministry of Foreign Affairs informed the diplomatic corps that they had to leave the territory of Korea because of the military situation. Meanwhile, rumors emerged that parachutists landed 40 kilometers away from the diplomats. The North Korean authorities could not provide any vehicles to the Hungarians. Therefore, Sándor Simics sent the Hungarian females and the kids ahead in his Dodge passenger car. Later, the Chinese diplomats sent back one of their trucks for the Hungarian envoy, his staff and their belongings. Arriving at Manchuria on November 2, probably Andong in Liaoning province, the Korean and the Chinese officials were at a loss regarding the accommodation of the evacuated diplomatic corps. Therefore, the Hungarians faced an odyssey of five days in Manchuria, covering 520 kilometers and

---

2) Karády, *Magyar sebész...*, 12.

3) Report written on December 20, 1950, by the Hungarian envoy Sándor Simics. MNL XIX-J-14 box no. 1.

crossing two rivers without any bridges. The cars got stuck in the cold water, so the passengers had no choice but to leave the flooded vehicles and cross the river, carefully walking on the stones of the riverbed.[4)]

As for the Hungarian political leader, the chief physician and Captain Moon Ho who had left for Manpho to find the Hungarian envoy came back to Jian on November 4 and said that the envoy was still staying in Korea, although it was not true. This wrong information was also mentioned in Karádi's recollections, stating that the envoy and the legation's first secretary, Mária Balog, arrived in Jian directly from Manpho on November 6.[5)] The diplomats did arrive on that day from inland Manchuria, not from Manpho. According to the envoy's report to Budapest, Jian was not prepared for housing the whole diplomatic corps. However, the North Korean deputy minister of foreign affairs informed the corps that the military situation had changed and they could return to Korea. Sándor Simics wrote in his report that the Soviet diplomats were the first to cross the Amnok (Yalu) River to go to Manpho on November 7, and the other missions followed them to observe their newly designated residential area. On the following day, the missions moved to Manpho – this time permanently –, and the Soviet embassy organized a reception for them to commemorate the 33rd anniversary of the 'Great October Socialist Revolution' which was one of the biggest holiday in the socialist countries. According to Sándor Simics, the diplomatic corps were accommodated in small 'Japanese style' houses made of wood and traditional paper without any thermal insulation. The diplomats suffered from the cold, so they tried to build simple stoves in their rooms.[6)]

---

4) Report written on December 20, 1950, by the Hungarian envoy Sándor Simics. MNL XIX-J-14 box no. 1.

5) Karády, *Magyar sebész…*, 13.

6) Report written on December 20, 1950, by the Hungarian envoy Sándor Simics. MNL XIX-J-14 box no. 1.

Turning back to the Hungarian medical team, on November 12 at dawn, the aforementioned physician, Dr. Remete who also served as the party secretary of the medical team, went back to the North Korean border to check the whereabouts of their X-ray machine and the other equipment which had been sent to the border region from Yangdok. When he left for North Korea, the border region seemed peaceful, but four-engine aircrafts appeared soon, initiating a large-scale bombing over Manpho. The Hungarians were worried about Dr. Remete especially when, due to the napalm bombs, a fast-spreading fire started. Finally, the physician got back to Jian in the evening and explained to his colleagues that he spent the day in a small village on the outskirts of Manpho. He used the chimneys that remained intact as a shelter to protect himself from the bullets. Two days later, on the morning of November 14, the Hungarians were about to leave their barrack in Jian and move toward inland Manchuria. However, they could not depart as planned: although they were in Chinese territories, a bombardment began over Jian. According to Karádi, the local anti-aircraft guns shot two aircrafts, making them crash into the neighboring villages. After the bombardments, at 6 o'clock in the evening, the Hungarian medical team was able to leave Jian and take a train at the local railway station. The travel to the city of Tonghua located only 90 kilometers away from Jian took 12 hours due to the war in the neighboring country. Upon arrival in Tonghua, the medical team was transferred to a barrack where all of them were given warm military uniforms and winter caps. At that time, Karádi was seriously ill, suffering from typhoid fever, and two of the Hungarians had to constantly look after her. At 8:15 a.m. on the following morning, the medical team left Tonghua for Mukden (today's Shenyang) by train. However, Karádi and the two Hungarians escorting her arrived late at the railway station, and they missed the train. Captain Moon Ho who also fell behind tried to obtain a car to follow the train with the

Hungarians, but eventually, due to Karádi's poor physical condition, all of them stayed in Tonghua. Finally, they reached Mukden by the car of the Hungarian Embassy in Beijing. Karádi was hospitalized immediately, and later she spent three weeks in a hospital in Beijing before she was sent back to Hungary.[7]

The medical team spent the second half of November in Mukden. Examining one of the archive sources, the aforementioned Dr. Remete went back again to Manpho on November 28 probably to search for their medical equipment that was left behind.[8] At that time, Manpho was bombed several times, and the houses of the Chinese, Mongolian, and Czechoslovakian diplomatic missions burned down. It was only a matter of time until the Hungarian mission was set on fire. According to the diplomatic report, the fire was extinguished by the legation's first secretary, the aforementioned Maria Balog, and two male employees. Due to the difficult circumstances, the Hungarian envoy, Sándor Simics went back to Manchuria to purchase some food.[9] The chief physician wrote in his diary that the envoy visited them in Mukden on December 1, only three days before their moving to Changchun city.[10]

---

7) Karády, *Magyar sebész…*, 13-14.

8) Diary of Ottó Diner.

9) Report written on December 30, 1950, by the Hungarian envoy Sándor Simics. MNL XIX-J-14 box no. 1.

10) Diary of Ottó Diner.

V. The second group in the Far East. Experiences in Manchuria

Changchun was previously the capital city of the Japanese puppet state Manchukuo (1932-1945). Therefore, especially in contrast to the Korean battlefield, it was rather modern and developed. The Hungarian medical team was transferred to a local hospital in Changchun where rumors were spreading about undisciplined Korean patients having rebelled against the hospital's rules at least three times. According to the rumors, the patients beat the Korean staff of the hospital with their crutches and snuck out to visit some local pubs and the cinema. Nevertheless, the Hungarian medical team managed to keep the discipline: the leaders of the patient gangs were appointed as room chiefs who were responsible for the order in their rooms.[1] Meanwhile, in December 1950, the Soviet and the Chinese embassies moved back to the reoccupied Pyongyang, but the other missions stayed around Manpho city in the Northern part of the country. According to the archive reports, it seems that Sándor Simics was one of the envoys who thought that it would be better to operate the legation in Chinese territory. Finally, after dozens of extreme experiences, the envoy left North Korea in January 1951 and moved back to Hungary, and the above-mentioned Mária Balog was promoted to charge d'affaires at the legation in North Korea.[2]

1) Reminiscences of János Dénes, 8-9.

2) Report written on February 4, 1951, by the Hungarian charge d'affaires Mária Balog. MNL XIX-J-14 box no. 1. 1-59.

The second Hungarian medical team left for Manchuria on February 11, 1951; their train departed from the Budapest Nyugati Railway Station at 11 o'clock in the evening. According to the reminiscences of military surgeon, Dr. János Dénes (1914–1985), the team arrived at the Hungarian-Soviet border in the following morning.[3] At the border station, the medical team transferred to a train for Moscow. Four people were seated in each cabin and the team enjoyed the on-board good food and drink services while the train crossed the Carpathian Mountains. It is interesting to mention that only 6-7 years before, the territory was the battlefield of the Soviet army and the Nazi Germany. The train arrived in Lvov in the evening, where one of the team members, who had taken care of the customs on the border and then took a plane for Lvov, joined the team again. In Kiev, the weather was quite cold, the temperature was minus 10 degrees Celsius, and in Moscow it was even colder, around minus 18 degrees Celsius. The team was greeted by Hungarian and North Korean diplomats at the railway station and they were transported to the Savoy Hotel which was one of the most prestigious hotels in the Soviet capital. During the journey, Dr. Dénes suffered from fever due to the typhus vaccine that he had received earlier. The Hungarian surgeon was brought to a local medical station where he was examined, and he was surprised since, despite the fact that physicians never asked for money among each other in the socialist countries, he had to pay for the examination. Meanwhile, the other members of the Hungarian team enjoyed their time in Moscow. They visited the Kremlin and the Bolshoi Theater. In the evening, the whole group participated in a banquet dinner of the North Korean Embassy, which was held in the Metropol Hotel.[4] The charge d'affaires of the Hungarian

---

3) Reminiscences of János Dénes.

4) Reminiscences of János Dénes, 2-3.

Embassy in Moscow wrote in his report that the group's supplier bought some special goods in the Soviet capital which they wanted to use in East Asia. Those were a high performance radio receiver and a camera with magnesium flash.[5)]

In the evening of February 18, 1951, the Hungarians continued their journey, taking a train at Yaroslavsky railway station, and the North Korean financial minister, Choi Chang-ik who was on his way to Budapest, greeted them on the platform.[6)] The aforementioned surgeon, Dr. Dénes, explained in his reminiscences that the journey was very comfortable in their brand new East Germany-made sleeping car, emphasizing that even on-board music broadcast was available. The Hungarians enjoyed the luxurious service in the dining car; they ate a lot of Soviet caviar, salmon and beefsteak, and drank local beer. Passing the city of Gorky (today's Nizhny Novgorod), the Ural Mountains, the Lake Baikal and the town of Chita, the train finally reached the Soviet-Chinese border. However, the Hungarians delayed the transfer to the connecting train to Manchuria. Therefore, they were accommodated in a local hotel in the Chinese border city of Manzhouli. It was the first time when the physicians had the opportunity to experience Chinese gastronomy and observe various Chinese porcelains. According to Dr. Dénes, it was also their first time to use squat toilets.[7)]

In the following morning, the Hungarians looked around the

---

5) Report written on February 21, 1951 by the Hungarian charge d'affaires to Moscow, Gyula Andrásfi. MNL XIX-J-1-k box no. 12. 28/c.

6) Choi Chang-ik (1896-1957): Korean communist politician. He was born in Onsong county near the Chinese border in the Northern part of the Korean Peninsula. Choi was an independence activist during the Japanese colonial rule and was arrested several times. He spent the last years of the colonial rule in China, and later, in the North Korean regime, he became the leader of the faction which collected the communists who had previously lived in exile in China. However, in 1956, as a supporter of de-Stalinization, he turned against Kim Il-sung. Choi was purged and transferred to the directorial post of a pig farm. Soon after, he was arrested and probably executed.

7) Reminiscences of János Dénes, 4-6.

city which they found remarkably dirty. All of the local residents were wearing quilted coats and sneakers. The physicians visited the local market where peanuts, green figs and frozen fish were sold. Dr. Dénes emphasized in his recollections that the commerce in the markets belonged to the private sector at that time, and they heard rumors that private land properties were still existing in the Southern part of China despite the socialist political system. It was a surprising moment for the Hungarians when they met another Hungarian man in a small shoemaker's shop in town. He was previously an Austro-Hungarian soldier who got captured by the Tsarist Russian troops during the WW1, transferred to a Siberian camp and eventually decided to stay in the Far East. He had absolutely no idea what was happening in Hungary at that time.[8] The medical team continued its journey toward inland Manchuria on the board of a Chinese train which was dirtier than the Soviet express. However, the Chinese trains were amazingly punctual at that time. It could be the aftermath of the Japanese colonial rule over Manchuria which was previously a puppet state under the name of Manchukuo (1932-1945). Dr. Dénes emphasized that from the border, the Hungarians were escorted by Chinese security officials who held guns under their outerwear. As it was explained later, the local residents in Manchuria sometimes attacked and stabbed Europeans simply because they believed that the foreigners were Soviets. It is probable that the traditional Sino-Soviet rivalry had already existed at that time despite the so-called 'fraternal friendship' between the communist empires. Therefore, the security officials escorted the Hungarian team during their entire stay in

[8] It is interesting to mention that in the late 1930's, a Hungarian lawyer, István Mezey, who was the founder of the Hungarian Nippon Association, traveled around Japan and Machukuo. He published a book about his journey, in which he mentioned that some of the former Austro-Hungarian soldiers were living in Manchukuo at that time. Source: Mezey, István: *Az igazi Japán*. (The real Japan – in Hungarian) Budapest: Magyar Nippon-Társaság Kiadása, 1939.

A street view in the Manchurian city of Changchun, the photo was taken by a member of the Hungarian medical team
(Semmelweis Medical History Museum, Budapest)

The building of the hospital in Changchun, the workplace of the first and the second Hungarian groups
(Semmelweis Medical History Museum, Budapest)

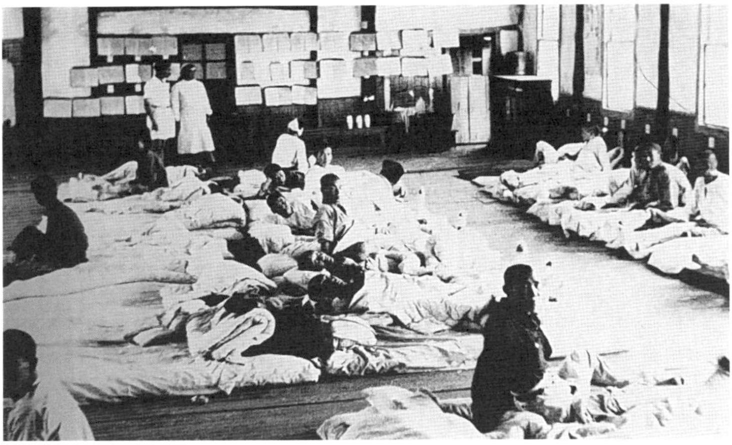

Patients in the hospital in Changchun, the photo was taken by a member of the Hungarian medical team
(Semmelweis Medical History Museum, Budapest)

Manchuria.[9)]

At 5:30 a.m. on February 28, 1951, the second Hungarian medical team arrived in Changchun city. The physicians were greeted at the railway station by Korean girls who gave them flowers and sang a song. Mária Balog, the charge d'affaires of the Hungarian legation which was in Manpho city at that time, also traveled to Changchun for the greetings. Furthermore, the Korean director of the Hungarian hospital, Dr. Ri Kang-guk, was there to welcome the team. The newcomers were accommodated in the most prestigious hotel of the city. The rooms were equipped with bathrooms, and international dishes were available in the restaurant. However, the whole building was uncared-for and quite dirty. Right after the newcomer colleagues' arrival, the members of the first medical team introduced the hospital to them, but they were shocked by the dirty environment. However, as it was explained

9) Reminiscences of János Dénes, 6-7, 14.

The aftercare hospital in Changchun, the photo was taken by a member of the Hungarian medical team
(Semmelweis Medical History Museum, Budapest)

to the second team, the hospital was the cleanest one in Manchuria at that time, and the first Hungarian group had started their service in the hospital under much worse circumstances.[10)]

Dr. Dénes explained in his reminiscences that the hospital was only a four-minute walk from their hotel. The Korean patients kindly greeted the newcomer physicians by clapping their hands despite their previous rebellions against the hospital's rules. Seemingly, they respected the European physicians but not the Korean paramedics of the hospital. Before starting their daily service, the newcomers made excursions in the city a couple of times and discovered that it has two parts: a Japanese and a Chinese one. The newly built Japanese part had long avenues, parks and beautiful, imposing buildings used by the state bureaucracy, some colleges and the military university of medical studies. The

10) Reminiscences of János Dénes, 7-8.

Dr. János Dénes, Military surgeon
(Semmelweis Medical History Museum, Budapest)

physicians visited a few state-owned department stores where they were surprised by the low prices and bought various porcelains, leather and ivory goods. The Hungarians observed that due to the lack of gasoline, only a very limited number of automobiles could be seen in the city. Moreover, there were also only a couple of tramcars. Therefore, the main transportation vehicles were the rickshaws. The Chinese part of the city was much simpler. One or two-storey houses were located along the streets with some bazaars and shanty buildings.[11)] As for the local clothing habit, Dr. Dénes mentioned that people in Changchun wore quilted clothes and sneakers. The surgeon also observed that the locals wore masks which were similar to what the physicians were using in the operating theatres to protect themselves from the dust.[12)]

In the evening of March 1, 1951, a large-scale banquet was held for the Hungarian medical team in their hotel, which was

11) Reminiscences of János Dénes, 8-11.

12) Reminiscences of János Dénes, 22.

One of the banquettes in Changchun which was held for the Hungarian medical team
(Semmelweis Medical History Museum, Budapest)

followed by a movie watching event and a dance party at the local Soviet-Chinese Club. On the following day, the wife of the Hungarian Ambassador to China arrived in Changchun to visit the physicians. Her arrival was an occasion for yet another banquet. However, the medical team felt that the new event was a waste of money. Dr. Dénes explained in his reminiscences that a huge amount of food was prepared for the event, and the guests were greeted in four languages; in Korean, in Chinese, in Russian and finally, in Hungarian. Nevertheless, the surgeon thought that it would have been much better to use the budget for other purposes, for example, for hospital expenses. Two days later, the Chinese side held a banquet for the Hungarians as well as the Korean and Soviet officials, where sixteen different dishes were served. However, the Hungarians felt that the series of the banquets was an exaggeration.[13)]

Although the medical team was located not very far from

13) Reminiscences of János Dénes, 8-11.

the Korean battlefield, they had very limited access to the news about the actual developments. Dr. Dénes mentioned that during the nights, some of the physicians were able to listen to the radio broadcast from Budapest with a high frequency receiver. However, it was hardly audible. The medical team usually listened to the Hungarian speaking program of the Radio of Moscow. For the physicians, writing letters forwarded by diplomatic couriers was the only way to communicate with their families. However, at first, the Hungarian Embassy in Beijing made a mistake and sent the letters with the courier to the Hungarian legation in Manpho, North Korea instead of Changchun. Therefore, the physicians had to wait weeks to get their letters back while the legation sent them back to Beijing, from where the Embassy forwarded them to Changchun. Meanwhile, the newcomers started their work in the hospital; each newcomer joined a colleague from the first group and got acquainted to their patients. Each physician had a Korean medical assistant who bandaged the wounds, gave the injections and managed the administration. The assistants also served as interpreters; all of them spoke either English, German or Russian. The only well-experienced Korean doctor in the hospital was an elderly man, Dr. Nam who was always called only by his family name. He and his team were responsible for the blood transfusions around 15-20 times a day. The donors were the staff members of the hospital. After completing the transfer of job responsibilities, the first group of the Hungarian medical teams headed back to Hungary on March 12, 1951. A few days later, a new group of injured Koreans - around 70 people in bad condition - arrived at the hospital. The physicians separated them according to the type of their injuries: upper limb cases, lower limb cases, abdomen and chest cases, and neurosurgery cases. The aforementioned Dr. Dénes was responsible for the abdomen and chest injuries, and he explained in his recollections that during the treatment of the patients, the Hungarian physicians actively co-worked with their Korean medic assistants. According to Dr. Dénes, one of the patients had two holes in his chest, and it was possible to see through the man's body who was still alive. Another person was shot in the abdomen and surprisingly survived the transportation from the battlefield to Changchun. However, seriously wounded people with those kinds of injuries usually died on the battlefield due to the lack of field medical treatment. Despite the careful therapies, some of the patients passed away, and they were buried in Changchun. Based on the traditional Korean way of thinking, their faces were placed to the direction of the Korean Peninsula. Meanwhile, there were some positive changes in the Hungarian hospital: due to a new shipment from Hungary, all of the sheets and blankets were changed and the patients received new pajamas and negligees. Wearing their new and clean clothes, the patients started to pay more attention to the cleanliness of their rooms. Finally, the building of the hospital was whitewashed. As Dr. Dénes noted in his reminiscences, the institution reached the level of an average countryside hospital in Hungary.[14)]

Meanwhile, on April 4, 1951, the Hungarians held a reception for the Korean, Chinese and Soviet officials on the occasion of one of the Hungarian national holidays of the socialist era. For the event, the medical team ordered catering for 150 people and a Hungarian dramatic movie was screened. The movie titled 'Talpalatnyi föld' ('Land of a human') is a sad story taking place in 1930. It is about a peasant girl who has to marry with a wealthy man in order for her parents to be able to pay back their debt, but she finally escapes from her own wedding with her true love. However, the couple struggles to get by, and eventually, the girl's lover even gets involved in a murder. The movie which shows minor parallels with the classic Korean silent movie 'Arirang'

14) Reminiscences of János Dénes, 12-19.

earned great recognition among the Korean and Chinese audience.[15] It is interesting to mention that three days later, the same movie was shown in Manpho, North Korea, at the event of the Hungarian legation in which diplomats from the other missions and Soviet citizens participated.[16]

Turning back to the Hungarian medical team, they were once visited by a Chinese elite medical group form Beijing. The members of the group were volunteer surgeons, urologists and orthopedics and spent only a short time in Changchun. The Hungarians were amazed by their professionalism; all of them had studied in America through various scholarships. Later, a Chinese physician who also studied in America suggested a new surgical technique to Dr. Dénes, which was already a routine procedure in America at that time, and offered him an American field anesthesia machine brought from the Korean battlefield to be used for their next operation.[17] In mid-April 1951, the Hungarians visited the hospital in Changchun where the aforementioned Chinese volunteer physicians worked temporarily. The Hungarians were surprised at the fact that the vast majority of the treated people in the hospital were paying patients, which was quite unusual in a socialist country; as mentioned above, Dr. Dénes had been shocked in Moscow when he had to pay for an examination at a local medical station. Seemingly, despite the communist ideology, some traces of capitalism could be discovered in the red empires at that time.[18] It also should be added that, in the People's Republic of China which was established only one and a half year earlier, the tradition of the feudalism still existed. The group's supplier, Tibor Heltai, wrote in

---

15) Reminiscences of János Dénes, 19.

16) Report written on April 8, 1951, by the Hungarian charge d'affaires Mária Balog. MNL XIX-J-14 box no. 1. 1-59.

17) Reminiscences of János Dénes, 13-17.

18) Reminiscences of János Dénes, 19.

his diary that he was invited to the house of a wealthy Chinese man in Andong where he lived with his five wives. Despite the campaign against the polygamy which was initiated by the All-China Women's Federation, this practice was still frequently observed in the countrysides of China in the early 1950s.[19)]

Meanwhile, the Hungarian Ambassador from Beijing, Emánuel Safrankó, visited the Hungarian medical team in Changchun.[20)] The diplomat gave 500 Hungarian forints to each members of the group to buy summer clothes before their move to North Korea. At that time, the average monthly salary in Hungary was around 1,000 forints. Therefore, 500 forints was not a small amount particularly if one regards the prices in China in the early 1950s. A set of Chinese-made clothes cost around 100 forints, and a pair of summer shoes could be bought for 30 forints. The physicians almost fell into temptation, looking at imported luxury fountain pens and Swiss-made wristwatches available for 240 forints.[21)] This episode also confirms that some capitalist elements did exist at that time despite the political system.

---

19) Diary of Tibor Heltai, 9-11. HM HIM MN Kgy: C-305 Hungarian Ministry of Defense, Military History Archive (Hungary, Budapest)

20) Safrankó, Emánuel (1890-1965): Hungarian communist, diplomat. He was born in the Northern part of Hungary and joined the leftist movement at a young age. In the early 1920s, he lived in Czechoslovakia where he was among the founding members of the Czechslovakian Communist Party. In 1929, he moved to the Soviet Union and returned to Hungary after the WW2. As a veteran communist cadre, he became the Ambassador of Hungary to Sofia, then to Beijing and finally, to East Berlin.

21) Reminiscences of János Dénes, 22.

VI. Moving back to Korea

In the second year of the Korean War, some other Central and Eastern European countries decided to send medical teams to the Korean War. The military surgeon Dr. János Dénes mentioned in his reminiscences that in April 1951, a medical team from Romania arrived in Changchun with eight physicians and twelve paramedics.[1] Comparing some of the archive sources about them, a few pieces of contradictory information were found; a Hungarian diplomatic report wrote that along with the eight physician, sixteen nurses served in the medical team. However, only one of them was a qualified professional.[2] The team was sent under the umbrella of the International Red Cross. However, they had absolutely no idea where they were supposed to go exactly. The Romanian physicians visited the Hungarian hospital and were delighted to see its cleanliness. In May 1951, the Romanians moved to a seaside village, 20 kilometers away from Shinuiju where they received a bigger building to accommodate and treat severely wounded patients and also some small Korean houses in the neighboring villages. According to the Hungarian diplomatic report, the Romanian team faced difficulties because of the lack of gypsum and bandage. The food supply of the hospital was delivered from Beijing.[3] Back then, the Czechoslovakian and Bulgarian governments also sent medical

---

1) Reminiscences of János Dénes, 21.

2) Report written on July 31, 1951, by the Hungarian envoy Károly Pásztor. MNL XIX-J-1-k box no. 12. 28/c.

3) Report written on July 31, 1951, by the Hungarian envoy Károly Pásztor. MNL XIX-J-1-k box no. 12. 28/c.

teams to North Korea, but the relations between the Eastern European hospitals remained superficial due to the long distance between their institutions.

Meanwhile, the Hungarian medical team observed the May Day celebrations in Changchun. There was a huge military parade and a marching by the local residents – Dr. Dénes compared its size to the Rio Carnival. In the evening, the mayor of the city held a reception for the physicians at a former Japanese Shinto shrine. It was followed by a half-an-hour-long firework which they watched from the top of an office building. Their relation with the mayor was very good. Therefore, the mayor invited them for a mallard hunt. The excursion was made on the last Sunday of May when the Hungarians and the officials of the city left for the neighboring mountains by cars. The roads in the countryside were in extremely bad shape, but the Hungarians enjoyed their time spent at the bank of a dammed lake which provided the city with water.[4)]

Finally, in the second half of June 1951, the Hungarian medical team moved back from Manchuria to North Korea. According to an archive diplomatic report of the Hungarian legation, the moving was initiated by the North Korean government.[5)] Dr. Dénes explained in his reminiscences that the Hungarian and Korean staff traveled by cars, and the boxes with their belongings and equipment were carried by a freight train. The aforementioned supplier, Tibor Heltai, also traveled by that train and wrote about all of his experiences in details in his diary. When he was walking past an express train which was ready to depart for Moscow in Mukden station on June 22, he saw some European men looking out the windows of the express train. When one of them saw Heltai, he said the followings in Hungarian language to his mates: 'Look, that guy!

4) Reminiscences of János Dénes, 23, 25.

5) Report written on July 24, 1951, by the Hungarian envoy Károly Pásztor. MNL XIX-J-14 box no. 1. 1-59.

He is wearing a Hungarian military raincoat!'[6] Hearing this, Heltai thought that the men on the train were probably Hungarians, but some Chinese guards on the train ordered the Europeans to stay away from the windows. Heltai asked a North Korean officer who they were, because they looked like captives of the Chinese military. It became clear that the people on the train were the Hungarian members of the French Foreign Legion and prisoners who were being transfered by the Communist forces from the Vietnamese battlefield. The men were deported back to Hungary via China and the Soviet Union.[7]

The Hungarian medical team crossed the Amnok (Yalu) River from Andong to Shinuiju on a temporary bridge; due to the bombardments, there was no lighting on either side of the river. The Korean staff were so happy and emotional when they finally crossed the river and reached Korean territory that they even shed some tears. The same was written in the diary of Tibor Heltai. The North Korean soldiers on the freight train which carried the equipment of the hospital buried their faces and cried when the train crossed the river.[8] Dr. Dénes and his fellow medical workers were temporarily accommodated in a villa in Shinuiju and then they continued their journey to Pyongyang on the board of three trucks. The roads were full of bomb craters, and during the nights, the traffic was very busy. Along the road to Pyongyang, the Hungarians saw the destroyed villages and their ruins. Finally, the team arrived in the North Korean capital on the early morning of June 26, 1951. Dr. Dénes continued his way on the same day to the designated place of the Hungarian hospital. It was in Mangyongdae which is known to be the birthplace of Kim Il-sung.[9] At that time, Kim's

---

6) Diary of Tibor Heltai, 2-3.

7) Diary of Tibor Heltai, 3.

8) Diary of Tibor Heltai, 13.

9) Reminiscences of János Dénes, 27, 29.

aunt was still living there, and later she visited the Hungarian hospital at least once.[10)]

Unlike the journey of the medical teams, the freight train went through more difficulties on its way, which made it reach the destination a lot later. As Tibor Heltai wrote in his diary, the train consisted of seven railroad cars including the five Chinese ammunition wagons connected in Andong by the order of the North Korean – Chinese headquarters. Moreover, a separate car loaded with a Chinese anti-aircraft unit was added on the back of the train to protect the train from the air raids. As described, the train was not carrying Humanitarian supplies only. However, it did not cause any problems as the train was not marked with the symbol of the International Red Cross. According to Heltai, they did not put the symbol on the top of the wagons because the train moved only during the nights when no one could see any.[11)] The train was guarded by a platoon of two North Korean soldiers. They sat on the top of the wagons together with Heltai. They crossed a hidden bridge of the Amnok (Yalu) River after midnight on June 24, 1951, which was located 10 kilometers Northeast from Andong and Shinuiju. Since the bridge was built slightly under the level of the water, it was not detected by the aircrafts. When the train received orders to cross the bridge, some other trains were waiting behind them to enter North Korea.[12)]

At that time, trains were operated only at night due to the air raids. The chimneys of the steam locomotives were covered with wet sacks in order to avoid the formation of sparks that could have been visible from the aircrafts. During the daytime, all of the trains were parked in one of the seven tunnels between the border and the

---

10) Report written on June 7, 1952, by the Hungarian envoy Károly Pásztor. MNL XIX-J-1-k box no. 12. 28/c.

11) Diary of Tibor Heltai, 15.

12) Diary of Tibor Heltai, 13.

Tibor Heltai, Hungarian supplier
(Semmelweis Medical History Museum, Budapest)

capital. In some of these tunnels were workshops operated for repairing the bombarded locomotives and wagons. At dawn on June 24, 1951, the train reached the first tunnel where two parallel tracks were built. After the train went into the tunnel, the anti-aricraft car was unbuckled from the back and camouflaged itself with green boughs at the entrance of the tunnel. The soldiers and the staff of the train washed themselves and their clothes in the neighboring stream in the morning and had compulsory sleep in the afternoon. The train continued to run only in the evening and stopped for a few minutes in the next tunnel to receive water into the locomotive. In the tunnel were three parallel tracks with equipment of overhauls. Heltai also saw a moving crane which could lift the locomotives.[13]

When the freight train loaded with the equipment of the Hungarian hospital was attacked for the first time after midnight on June 25, 1951, the driver of the locomotive slammed the brakes on

13) Diary of Tibor Heltai, 26.

several times. Since the pilot of the attack aircraft failed to perceive the real speed of the train, the bombs fell onto the ground much ahead of the train. Soon after, they faced a new obstacle. They had to cross a bridge over a valley which had been damaged but repaired only partially. The five Chinese ammunition wagons seemed too heavy to cross the bridge. Therefore, the staff wanted to unbuckle the five wagons to leave them behind with the anti-aircraft unit. They wanted to run the train to the next tunnel first, and then the locomotive could come back for the five wagons. However, the driver of the locomotive was strongly opposed to this idea because he was sure that he would not be able to make one more round trip to the next tunnel before the sunrise. The staff asked all of the soldiers to get off the train and cross the bridge on foot while the driver ran the train to the other side very slowly. However, the commander of the Chinese soldiers in the ammunition wagons insisted that his soldiers remain on board. After all, the train crossed the bridge with its full staff on. According to the diary of Tibor Heltai, the temporarily repaired bridge made crackling sounds under the weight of the train which moved very slowly. Heltai saw wrecks of a train deep in the water which had fallen into the river probably during an air raid. To relieve the tension, the Hungarian supplier started to sing some revolutionary songs loudly, including *The Internationale* and the *Workers of Vienna*. The Koreans and the Chinese joined in singing in their native languages until the train crossed the bridge safely.[14)]

Before sunrise, the freight train arrived safely at the next tunnel. As Tibor Heltai wrote in his diary, the staff called the North Korean – Chinese headquarter on the radio to ask for permission to leave the ammunition wagons behind in the tunnel and carry them to the destination by a different locomotive later. However, the

---

14) Diary of Tibor Heltai, 27-29.

proposal was rejected. The staff also suggested connecting empty cars between the last freight car of the hospital to the first ammunition wagon in order to save the train from the potential explosion of the ammunition, which was also rejected. Therefore, the train continued to move to Pyongyang in the evening of June 26, 1951 as it was originally planned. After dark, the aircrafts showed up and dropped the flash bombs all over the places. It was only a matter of time before the train became a target. Two fighter planes attacked the train immediately and the Chinese anti-aircraft unit on the back started to counter-attack the planes. Heltai who was sitting on the top of a car instinctively took his pistol out and shot toward aircrafts. Of course, he was well aware that the bullets from his pistol could not make any damage on the planes. One of the two fighters flew away while the other continued to attack. It set fire to the last freight car and the first ammunition wagon. The Korean and the Chinese soldiers reacted very quickly; unbuckled the four intact ammunition wagons and the car of the anti-aircraft unit from the back of the train immediately. Then, they unbuckled the last freight car and the first ammunition wagon which were burning like a torch. The two burning cars stopped moving on the track and exploded. One of the fighters came back to observe the detonation and the Chinese anti-aircraft unit shot the plane down.[15)]

The damage of the railroad was repaired quickly by the local residents. The train moved backward for the four intact ammunition wagons. Before sunrise, the train arrived at the next tunnel where the anti-aircraft unit was unbuckled again to protect the tunnel's entrance. Tibor Heltai wrote in his diary that he was skeptical about the possibility to reach their destination alive. All of a sudden, large-scale air raids started again and a large amount of carbon monoxide was accumulated in the tunnel where two other trains

---

15) Diary of Tibor Heltai, 38-40.

were waiting for sunset. The only person who sensed danger was the Hungarian supplier. The Chinese soldiers in the four ammunition wagons collapsed due to the carbon monoxide. Heltai carried the soldiers outside, but eventually he also fainted. He regained his consciousness after a North Korean military physician gave him an injection. The carbon monoxide killed one of the Chinese soldiers while all the others survived thanks to Heltai's speedy rescue. The staff called the North Korean – Chinese headquarter on the radio and informed them what had happened. The commander did not allow them to bury the dead soldier because a Chinese military prosecutor would visit the spot shortly to investigate the case.[16] The high level Chinese officers came in the afternoon on the same day and wanted to talk with the Hungarian supplier. According to Heltai's diary, he tried to wash his face before the talk. The Chinese officers smiled at him to express their gratitude for saving the lives of their soldiers.[17] Heltai received a Chinese war medal which allowed him to go to see movies free of charge in Beijing. He found it very useful as he had an official trip scheduled to Beijing. He was surprised at the fact that a Hungary-related West German musical film was also shown in the cinemas. It was 'The Csardas Princess', starring Marika Rökk, a Hungarian-born musical legend who was popular among the Germans during the Nazi era. The Hungarian supplier watched the movie three times to take full advantage of the opportunity.[18]

In the last evening, a separate locomotive came and carried away the ammunition wagons and the anti-aircraft unit. The freight train arrived in Pyongyang early in the morning. The staff saw dozens of destroyed houses, fallen trees and pylons. The aforementioned

---

16) Diary of Tibor Heltai, 43.

17) Diary of Tibor Heltai, 48.

18) Zoltán, János: *Add vissza az arcomat. Egy plasztikai sebész a koreai háborúban.* (Give back my face! A Plastic Surgeon in the Korean War – in Hungarian) Pusztazámor: DNM, 1996, 84-85.

Dr. Dénes and Major Hwang Su-bong were waiting for the train in the camouflaged station. They brought trucks to transfer the shipment to the hospital. However, since the city came under heavy bombardment in the morning, unloading the train was delayed. Heltai and two North Korean military physicians who were also on the train were sent in advance to Mangyongdae on a Willys jeep, a war booty from the American troops. On the way, the Hungarian supplier observed dozens of local residents who got injured from the previous bombardement. They got burned and shed bled. Heltai was shocked at the fact that the North Korean physicians remained in the car without any attempt to give first aid to the injured citizens.[19)]

---

19) Diary of Tibor Heltai, 48-50.

VII. The hospital in Mangyongdae

The designated place in Mangyongdae was not the best location for a hospital. It consisted of two stone buildings, probably used as a college previously, which were located on the top of a hill. Therefore, they could be easy targets for bombings. Nevertheless, Taedong River was near to the designated place. Therefore, the Hungarians enjoyed swimming in the hot summer weather. Dr. Dénes described in details how the tide changed the river; not only the direction of the down-stream changed, but also small islands emerged and disappeared again due to the tide. The physicians were visited by the newly appointed Hungarian envoy to North Korea, Károly Pásztor, who brought a great amount of food for the newcomers. The new envoy was a professional soldier and probably his profession was the main reason of his nomination. The tough circumstances of the war in North Korea were expected to be much more tolerable for a professional soldier than a civilian. The Hungarian legation had moved from Manpho to the neighborhood of the capital at that time, of which location is hardly identifiable. A report which was written later states that the legation was in the town of Sori.[1] Unlike the aforementioned report, the leader of the second group of the Hungarian medical teams wrote in his official report that the legation was on the Moranbong in Pyongyang.[2] However,

1) Report written by Dr. Béla Berényi, the leader of the fifth group of the Hungarian medical team. HM HIM MN Kgy: C-223

2) Report written by Dr. Bálint Sőrés, the leader of the second group of the Hungarian medical team. HM HIM MN Kgy: C-223

The main building of the Hungarian hospital in Mangyongdae
(Photo Archive of the Hungarian Ministry of Defense, Budapest)

Károly Práth, Hungarian envoy to Korea (in the middle with a necktie) visits the village of Oru-ri, one of the unit of the Hungarian hospital in the neighborhood of Mangyongdae
(Photo Archive of the Hungarian Ministry of Defense, Budapest)

the envoy wrote in his reminiscence letter decades later that the place was located 20-22 kilometers away from Pyongyang.[3] Despite the contradictory information, it seems that the legation was in the valley of the Sopho Mountain which is located 10 kilometers away from the capital. It was the same place where the vast majority of the foreign missions were settled at that time.[4]

Károly Pásztor had presented his letter of credentials to the nominal head of the North Korean state, Kim Du-bong, on June 15, 1951. According to the contemporary diplomatic report, the ceremony was held under quite unusual circumstances. The protocol chief of the North Korean foreign ministry picked up the envoy at the legation and escorted him to a village 25 kilometers east of Pyongyang where he presented the documents to Kim Du-bong. Then, they listened to the national hymns standing under the eaves of a small peasant house. After a short formal conversation, the envoy was urged to leave the village before the rainstorm approached.[5]

Turning back to Mangyongdae, the dangerous location of the hospital on the hilltop was mentioned in one of the diplomatic reports sent by the newly appointed Hungarian envoy to Budapest. Károly Pásztor wrote that he talked about it with health minister Yi Byeong-nam and commercial minister Chang Shi-woo who also served as the commander of the hinterland. All of them agreed that the place was a favorable location for a hospital in peacetime, but during the war, it could be an easy target. However, since the North Korean authorities could not find a better place for the institution, the Hungarians had to move there. The envoy was informed that the electric facilities and the water pipes were replaced in the venue,

---

3) Letter written on November 6, 1986, by the former Hungarian envoy Károly Pásztor. HM HIM MN Kgy: C-305

4) Email message sent on November 20, 2020, by the Russian Embassy in Pyongyang to the author.

5) Report written on June 17, 1951, by the Hungarian envoy Károly Pásztor. MNL XIX-J-14 box no. 1. 1-59.

Shell of an American Sherman tank in the neighborhood of the Hungarian hospital
(Semmelweis Medical History Museum, Budapest)

Shell of an American Sherman tank with Chinese soldiers in the neighborhood of the Hungarian hospital
(Photo Archive of the Hungarian Ministry of Defense, Budapest)

A picture of an overturned truck taken by a member of the Hungarian medical team
(Semmelweis Medical History Museum, Budapest)

but according to the reminiscences, it was probably false information.[6] It is important to mention that the envoy had mixed feelings after the talks with health minister Yi Byeong-nam. The minister said that he received a lot of letters from recovered North Korean soldiers who appreciated the work of the Hungarian medical team. However, Yi Byeong-nam was uncommunicative and refused to share basic information about the North Korean health situation with the envoy.[7]

In Mangyongdae, the danger of air attacks was not the only reason that reminded the Hungarians that they were on a battlefield. According to the recollections, the wreck of a totally burnt out Sherman tank was alongside the road near the hospital. Furthermore, while one of the North Korean soldiers who guarded the hospital

6) Report written on July 24, 1951, by the Hungarian envoy Károly Pásztor. MNL XIX-J-14 box no. 1. 1-59.

7) Report written on June 26, 1951, by the Hungarian envoy Károly Pásztor. MNL XIX-J-14 box no. 1. 1-59.

fell asleep during his duty, someone took the advantage and stole his rifle.[8] Particularly, this incident showed that 'white partisans' could be present in the hinterland. In the last days of June, Dr. Dénes heard from the Hungarian envoy that the Soviet Embassy, which was set up in camouflaged buildings in a hidden valley was bombarded during the previous night and some of the local staff lost their lives. According to Dr. Dénes, it was also an evidence of the 'white partisans' activity and probably the 'white partisans' were the ones who gave informations about the exact location of the Soviet Embassy to the Americans.[9] As it was mentioned above, the Soviet Embassy was in the valley of the Sopho Mountain at that time. The building of the Soviet mission was previously used by the Japanese Kwantung Army.[10]

As an addition to the dangerous circumstances, the installation of the hospital in the new location was a really difficult task. The trucks arrived with the equipment during the nights. However, one of the vehicles was struck by a bomb, leaving a Korean staff member and some Chinese soldiers dead. Another truck ran off the road into a ditch and it was very dangerous to unload the equipment; some of the locals even got injured in the process. A few days later, a traditional funeral was held for the Korean staff member, which was unusual for the Hungarians due to the rites, during which the Koreans places several kinds of food and chopsticks for the soul to be able to leave this world. Turning back to the hardships, electricity and running water were not available due to the destruction of basic infrastructure, and the physicians had to build a shelter for themselves. However, the situation was much more difficult in other hospitals in North Korea at that time. Some

---

8) Zoltán, *Add vissza az arcomat*, 65-66; Reminiscences of János Dénes, 31.

9) Reminiscences of János Dénes, 33.

10) Email message sent on November 20, 2020 by the Russian Embassy in Pyongyang to the author.

of the Hungarians visited another institute, which was mentioned as hospital No. 39 and faced terrible circumstances upon their arrival. According to some records, hospital No. 39 was extremely dirty with thousands of flies, the wounds were not bandaged, and basically all of their activities were disorganized. The Hungarians noticed that one Soviet adviser was working in the hospital, but he could not achieve any development on his own. Due to this situation, the newcomer Bulgarian medical team was eventually entrusted with the management of the hospital No. 39. Meanwhile, on July 12, 1951, the first patients arrived in the Hungarian hospital in Mangyongdae; partly from the frontline and partly from another hospital. Most of them were in bad condition, so it took 6 hours for the medical staff to treat and stabilize more than 50 patients.[11)]

As mentioned above, the central building in Mangyongdae was situated on a hilltop. The operating theatre, the intensive care unit, the X-ray and the lab were in the basement. The physicians also designated a separate space to be used as the safety operating theatre which was called 'tiger's cave' since it was a room dug into the rock. Furthermore, in the spirit of decentralization, some medical activities were outsourced to the neighboring villages. The patients were separated according to their injuries; the abdomen and chest wounded were treated in Nam-ri, the lower limb cases were treated 2 kilometers away in Seongsan-ri and the upper limb cases were medicated 5 kilometers away in Oru-ri. The patients were accommodated in peasant houses while the local residents were responsible for preparing their food from ingredients previously provided by the Hungarian hospital. In one of the villages, there was a Korean cultural ensemble of actors, dancers, singers and musicians. Sometimes, the Hungarians watched their rehearsals. Then, on August 2, 1951, the artists gave a performance to the

11) Reminiscences of János Dénes, 33, 34-35.

Colonel Dr. Ri Kang-guk, director of the Hungarian hospital greets the delegation of the Democratic Association of the Hungarian Females on September 12, 1951
(Photo Archive of the Hungarian Ministry of Defense, Budapest)

Hungarian physicians in the village of Oru-ri, the neighborhood of Mangyongdae
(Semmelweis Medical History Museum, Budapest)

Delegation from the village of Seongsan-ri gives some gifts to the Hungarian physicians in 1951
(Photo Archive of the Hungarian Ministry of Defense, Budapest)

physicians. The performance was watched by a contemporary VIP official, Park Jong-ae who was the chairperson of the Women's Association of the DPRK.[12)]

Despite the difficult circumstances, after their daily service, the physicians often swam in the Taedong River. During these occasions, Dr. Dénes noticed that the Korean nurses of the hospital also enjoyed the cool water, totally naked in front of others. However, the same nurses were very bashful in the everyday life in

---

12) Park Jong-ae (1907-?): Korean communist politician. She was born in Russia and joined the communist movement at a young age. She went back to the Korean Peninsula in 1931, but the Japanese authorities imprisoned her soon after. After 1945, she became the chairwoman of the Women's Association of the DPRK. She was a member of the domestic faction but had very close relations with the Soviet faction and the partisan faction led by Kim Il-sung as well. In 1966, she war purged and exiled to the provinces.

the hospital, and one of them who once had a bad stomach ache did not allow the doctors to see her belly during the examination due to her shyness. It was one of the contradictory elements of the Korean culture.[13] Turning back to the day offs, the physicians often made excursions to a tranquil village where they had the opportunity to sunbathe and have a bath in the mountain creek. Usually, the physicians had three-day-long vacations. Once, the Hungarians discovered a Buddhist monastery in the mountains in total isolation, not at all affected by the Korean War. Sometimes, the physicians made a visit to Pyongyang which was totally destroyed, leaving the government agencies no choice but to operate underground. However, the physicians got the opportunity to visit the Moranbong Hill for official reasons since the bunker deep under the hill was used for huge receptions and performances as well. On August 20, 1951, the Hungarian legation in Pyongyang held a reception in the underground space to commemorate the Hungarian national holiday. The physicians departed from Mangyongdae at 5 o'clock in the afternoon. However, the drive to the capital was difficult due to the bombardments. At the beginning of the event, five Korean employees from the hospital received Hungarian state awards and the institution's deputy director, Major Hwang Su-bong, gave a speech in Hungarian language. Not only the local diplomatic corps and the officials of the North Korean bureaucracy, but also the nominal head of the North Korean state, the aforementioned Kim Du-bong, participated in the reception. According to Dr. Dénes, the Hungarian envoy, Károly Pásztor, was very nervous because it was the first reception he organized, but eventually he was very happy because everything went smoothly. The catering offered various Hungarian specialties including Tokaji wine and Hungarian salami. Therefore, the participants were probably able to forget for a moment that

13) Reminiscences of János Dénes, 37.

they were in an underground bunker in a city under constant bombardments.[14)]

Dr. Dénes explained in his reminiscences that the difficult circumstances became even more challenging because of a natural disaster in the end of the summer of 1951. After the heavy rains, water flowed down from the mountains, causing the most serious flood on the Taedong River in 50 years, flooding all of the islands and the neighboring villages including the birthplace of Kim Il-sung. From the hilltop where the main buildings of the hospital were located, the Hungarians observed, how the peasant houses were washed away by the flood. The disaster happened suddenly. The small boats on the bank were carried away by the river, and many of the residents drowned because they could not escape. The Koreans emphasized that the flood caused more damage than did the war. Because of the natural disaster, the hospital faced several problems: due to the lack of gasoline, they could not use their generator for electricity, and their food supply was also running out. Basically, they received meat once a week, but due to the bad weather, the meat went bad during the transportation. Furthermore, the hospital's storage ran out of butter and sugar. The situation improved only in September when the physicians finally received boxes of sausages, cheese, and champagne.[15)] On the other hand, the Hungarian envoy wrote in his summary report that the circumstances were improved by the 'Soviet supply' which included meat, sugar and oil.[16)]

---

14) Reminiscences of János Dénes, 41, 44.

15) Reminiscences of János Dénes, 38, 42-44.

16) Report written on October 20, 1951, by the Hungarian envoy Károly Pásztor. MNL XIX-J-1-k box no. 12. 28/c.

VIII. Hungarian correspondent visits the hospital in Mangyongdae

In August 1951, the Hungarian daily *Szabad Nép* sent a correspondent to North Korea to report on the peace negotiations that opened in Kaesong. Tibor Méray, the young journalist, travelled to East Asia by airplane and tried to cross the Amnok (Yalu) River from Andong to Shinuiju on the board of a small ferry. However, due to the river's rapid flow, they were able to arrive at the Korean bank only on their second attempt. The temporary bridge which was used by the physicians one and a half month earlier was not crossable at the time. More than sixty years later, Tibor Méray told me that from the North Korean side of the river, he could not see a single town that was undamaged. The Soviet-made Pobeda passenger car, which carried not only the correspondent, but also the envoy and his staff, moved forward on a side road toward the town of Anju where they merged onto the main road to Pyongyang. In the capital, the correspondent was transferred to the huge bunker under the Moranbong Hill where the celebrations were held on the anniversary of the liberation from the Japanese rule. According to Méray, during the celebration, the participants heard massive explosions from above, and when they went upstairs, they saw that a huge bombardment had reached the capital. Dead bodies were scattered everywhere; the vast majority of them were women in white casual clothes.[1)]

---

1) The author's interview with Tibor Méray, who served as the Hungarian

Tibor Méray, Hungarian journalist, in the garden of the Hungarian legation
(From the collection of Tibor Méray)

The Hungarian journalist made a visit to the Hungarian hospital in Mangyongdae and wrote his experiences not only in his articles on the pages of *Szabad Nép*, but also in his propagandistic books dedicated to his observations in Korea. In his first article, he described that the physicians came together for a medical concilium in the morning, which was held outside the building under a huge tree. In the afternoon, the journalist discovered one of the neighboring villages where only injuries of the same kind were treated in the spirit of decentralization. He saw not only the peasant houses, but also the 'club' of the village where books, papers, radio, chess and table tennis were available for the recovering patients. Furthermore, the journalist emphasized that the Hungarian hospital was 'spick-and-span'. The final part of the article described the late evening of the busy day when the physicians who finished their duty

correspondent in North Korea during the Korean War. (Paris, December 16, 2012.)

for the day were singing Hungarian folk songs together in the Korean night, more than 10 thousand kilometers away from their homeland.[2] In one of his books, the correspondent wrote about some Korean children living in the neighboring villages who knew the word 'Szervusz' which is one of the most common Hungarian informal greetings. Tibor Méray also explained in details how the Hungarian hospital overcame the language barriers between the physicians and the Koreans. All the Hungarian doctors spoke at least one of the European languages: German, English or Russian. However, the Koreans spoke only Japanese apart from their mother tongue and only a few of them spoke German, English or Russian. According to the correspondent, this situation resulted in the use of a mixture of languages containing Hungarian, English, Korean and even some Russian words. However, some members of the local staff started to learn Hungarian and were able to speak it within quite a short time.[3] Later, the Hungarian journalist published a report in *Szabad Nép* describing the circumstances with graphic details regarding how the physicians performed surgeries during the continuous bombardments and how the injured women and children were dying in the Hungarian hospital.[4] The description was probably not far from reality. However, articles like this one were shocking for the relatives of the Hungarian physicians back in Hungary. The aforementioned military surgeon, Dr. János Dénes who finished his service in Korea in January 1952, mentioned in his recollections that the relatives were really worried for the doctors because of the articles.[5]

---

2) Méray, Tibor, "Rákosi Mátyás Kórház, Korea" (Mátyás Rákosi Hospital, Korea – in Hungarian) *Szabad Nép*, September 16, 1951.

3) Méray, Tibor: *Koreai jelentés*. (Report on Korea – in Hungarian) Budapest: Szikra, 1953, 132-163.

4) Méray, Tibor, "Sebesült asszonyok és gyermekek között" (Among injured women and children – in Hungarian) *Szabad Nép*, July 22, 1952.

5) Reminiscences of János Dénes, 48.

The writings of Tibor Méray became emblematic during the Korean War in Hungary. Later, the main topic of his articles was the 'American germ warfare' on the Korean battlefields. The allegation became the propaganda tool of the communist countries against the USA, but the idea of that accusation was likely to have originated from China. The Hungarian daily *Szabad Nép* wrote about the alleged germ warfare for the first time on May 11, 1951. The article published the statement of foreign minister Park Hon-yong who accused General Douglas MacArthur of ordering the 'mass production' of germ weapons in Japan. According to the article, the Americans spent 1,5 million yens for the weapons which they wanted to use against the DPRK. Park Hon-yong also mentioned that North Korea had written evidence of the American program; the documents were obtained by the Korean People's Army in Seoul.[6] However, after that statement, the allegation of the germ warfare could not be heard for several months and was only mentioned again in February 1952. At that time, Park Hon-yong announced that the enemy's aircrafts had dropped germs - plague and cholera - on the North Korean hinterland. Two days later, the Chinese premier Zhou Enlai repeated the accusation, too.

According to Tibor Méray, he was informed for first time about the deployment of the germ weapons on March 2, 1952. The North Korean Ministry of Health shared some detailed information with him, and he was taken to a laboratory where various insects were exhibited. According to the official explanation, the insects carried deadly bacteria. Four days later, on March 6, Chinese physicians showed up at the Hungarian hospital with dead flies which had been allegedly infected by bacterias. According to the official report on the activities of the Hungarian hospital, the 'agents of the imperialists' released a great number of infected flies

---

6) "Baktériumfegyver alkalmazása..." (Deployment of germ weapon – in Hungarian) *Szabad Nép*, May 11, 1951.

into the neighborhood of the hospital on March 15, which were soon found and burned by the Hungarians.[7] However, a few month later, three Hungarian physicians who were heading back to Hungary told the staff of the Hungarian Embassy in Beijing during a private conversation that they never saw any sign of germ weapons in Korea.[8]

Turning back to Tibor Méray, he was taken to Sono village at the Taedong riverbank where the first alleged attack had happened. The Hungarian journalist observed the piles of dead flies on the frozen riverside. According to the local residents, the flies were thrown down from American aircrafts. The North Korean authorities told the Hungarian correspondent that the Americans wanted to infect the reservoir of the capital city. According to Méray, the explanation and the circumstances were clear and convincing. Moreover, he was taken to a district in Pyongyang where he was informed that three local people had died due to alleged cholera infection.[9] Therefore, from the spring of 1952, the Hungarian journalist started to write dozens of articles about the germ warfare and the guiltiness of the Americans. The archive reports about the development of the Hungarian hospital state that there is also information that in January 1953, allegedly infected flies and butterflies were found around Oru-ri where one of the departments of the hospital was being operated.[10] However, if one thoroughly examines the archive newspapers, it can be noticed that the Soviet propaganda-machine had started to spread that allegation much earlier. Following a Soviet article which was written by the

---

7) Report written probably in late 1952 by the Hungarian physicians Dr. János Bonta and Dr. György Bálint. HM HIM MN Kgy: C-226

8) Report written on May 31, 1952, by the Hungarian Ambassador to Beijing Emánuel Safrankó. MNL XIX-J-1-k box no. 12. 28/c.

9) Méray, Tibor: *Egy és más*. (One and the other – in Hungarian) Budapest: Jószöveg Műhely Kiadó, 2012, 248–250.

10) Report written about the developments in the Hungarian hospital between November 1, 1952, and January 20, 1953. HIM MN Kgy: C-226

Communist Information Bureau, the Hungarian *Szabad Nép* published its first article about the 'American germ warfare-plans' already in July 1950. The article stated that eighteen Japanese germ experts who had participated in the Japanese germ warfare program during the WWII were brought to America to join the 'satanic laboratory' in Camp Detrick to create germ weapons against the socialist countries.[11)]

However, several negative experiences on the Korean battlefield and particularly the purge and execution of his Korean friend Seol Chung-sik led the Hungarian correspondent to a political turn. Tibor Méray became a supporter of the anti-Stalinist Hungarian prime minister who became the leader of the Hungarian revolution in October, 1956. After the repression of the revolution by the Soviet troops, the young journalist left Hungary and became one of the key figures of the Hungarian intellectual exile circle in Western Europe, and even after the fall of communism, he never returned permanently to Hungary.

---

11) "Az amerikai kannibálok..." (American cannibals – in Hungarian) *Szabad Nép*, July 20, 1950.

IX. Hungarian observations in the second year of the Korean War

One of the most detailed descriptions on the period when the Hungarian hospital was located in Mangyongdae and its neighborhood was given by plastic surgeon Dr. János Zoltán (1921-2011). He joined the Hungarian medical team in September 1951 and traveled to North Korea on the Trans-Siberian railway. The physician recalled a very interesting detail about the train trip from Beijing to North Korea: he and his colleagues traveled together with some young European men who spoke in Russian and wore civilian clothes. However, each of them carried a machine gun. They were most probably soldiers of a special Soviet military unit that was sent to North Korea.[1] It is interesting to mention that some other Hungarian sources also hinted at the Soviet presence in Manchuria and probably in North Korea at that time. A young Hungarian student, Barna Tálas, who was studying at the Tsinghua University in Beijing, made an important observation in the spring of 1951. He and his fellow students visited the palace museum in Beijing where they met a platoon; the soldiers wore the uniform of the so called 'Chinese People's Volunteers'. However, they did not look like Chinese people, and they spoke in Russian among each other. Their officer tried to prevent any conversation between the foreign students and the soldiers. When the accompanying teacher asked the officer about the nationality of the soldiers, he said that

---

1) Zoltán, *Add vissza az arcomat*, 51.

they were volunteers of the 'e-luo-si' (俄罗斯) ethnic minority from Xinjiang province. Probably, they were Soviet soldiers somewhere from the Central Asian republics.[2] The aforementioned military surgeon, Dr. Dénes, also mentioned an episode related to the soldiers in his reminiscence. He and his fellow medical workers visited a special Soviet hospital in a castle-like building which had previously been the court of Manchukuo; back then, the convicted were executed in the building's courtyard. The hospital was used by the Soviet pilots and the soldiers of the air defense units, who served in Manchuria at that time. It was clean and well-equipped, but only a few patients were treated there.[3]

Turning back to the journey of plastic surgeon Dr. Zoltán, from the Chinese-Korean border city of Andong, the Hungarian plastic surgeon and his fellow travelers continued their trip by truck which was sent by the Hungarian legation in Pyongyang. The truck crossed the Amnok (Yalu) River on a partially destroyed bridge on which wooden boards were installed between the intact pillars. However, Dr. Zoltán wrote in his reminiscences that there was another bridge, 10 kilometers northeast of Andong. That bridge was built slightly below the surface of the water to be hidden from the bombardments, and it was hard to discover even at low tide. According to Dr. Zoltán, he and his fellows traveled on the truck's platform with pistols in their hands given to them by the Hungarian driver. They were told to indicate with a shot if they see any military aircrafts. When they did see one, the driver immediately stopped the truck, and everybody tried to find a shelter.[4] It is interesting to mention that from the autumn of 1951, not only

---

2) Tálas, Barna: *Egy Kína-kutató magyar diplomata emlékei a XX. század második feléből.* (Reminiscences of a Hungarian sinologist diplomat from the second half of the 20th century – manuscript in Hungarian), 206. Institute of Political History (Hungary, Budapest)

3) Reminiscences of János Dénes, 24-25.

4) Zoltán, *Add vissza az arcomat*, 54-55.

bombardments, but also fights between aircrafts could be seen over Korea. The aforementioned Dr. Dénes mentioned in his reminiscences that he once saw a burning aircraft crash.[5]

On November 7, 1951, a commemorative event for the 34th anniversary of the 'Great October Socialist Revolution' was held in the Hungarian hospital, which was one of the biggest holidays in the socialist countries at that time. Not only the local staff, but also the representatives of the neighboring villages were rewarded with small gifts by the Hungarians. The Koreans were very satisfied with the gifts and all of the participants enjoyed the dinner together. At that time, some of the physicians moved to Seongsan-ri, a village 2 kilometers away from Mangyongdae where they found a better house for sleeping. In the traditional Korean kitchen which was located next to the rooms, the Hungarians could boil some water to bath in a tub. It was a rare opportunity during the war in North Korea to wash with hot water in a bath tub.[6] The aforementioned plastic surgeon, Dr. Zoltán, once observed that the Korean nurses washed their hair with icy water in the rear garden of the hospital despite the frosty cold weather of winter.[7] At that time, the younger sister of Major Hwang Su-bong, Hwang Myung-sun, also worked in the hospital as an operating room nurse. According to the reminiscence, the physicians gave her a nickname, 'Nightingale' ('Csalogány' in Hungarian) because she was very good at singing. Later, Hwang was sent to Budapest to study music at the Liszt Academy.[8]

---

5) Reminiscences of János Dénes, 46.

6) Reminiscences of János Dénes, 49.

7) Zoltán, *Add vissza az arcomat*, 107.

8) However, during her stay in Budapest, she got married to one of her Chinese classmates. After the purge of her brother, she decided not to return to North Korea, and the couple left for China. Zoltán, *Add vissza az arcomat*, 103-105.

The bunker of the hospital in Mangyongdae
(Semmelweis Medical History Museum, Budapest)

Dr. Lajos Sándor and Dr. György Bálint, members of the third group, on the way to their workplace in the neighboring village. Kim Hae-jae, a local employee in the middle of the picture
(Photo Archive of the Hungarian Ministry of Defense, Budapest)

Members of the Hungarian medical team are getting on a truck in Mangyongdae. The picture was taken probably in the winter of 1951
(Semmelweis Medical History Museum, Budapest)

Dr. Dénes explained that in the wintertime, some of the physicians took their days off and spent time at the Hungarian legation of which exact location is still unknown. Dr. Dénes wrote the the place was located in a nice valley among pine forests which used to be known as a 'romantic place' decades earlier, where wealthy Koreans spent time with their mistresses. It is assumed that it was in the valley of the Sopho Mountain.[9] The legation was in a villa building and there was a small outbuilding in its garden where the physicians were accommodated during their visits. However, once, the neighborhood was bombarded and the small building partly collapsed while the physicians were having dinner in the main building of the legation. Despite the incident, Dr. Dénes and his colleague spent their day off at the legation in the early winter in 1951. According to his reminiscence, they left the hospital at dawn

---

9) Email message sent on November 20, 2020, by the Russian Embassy in Pyongyang to the author.

and arrived in the legation at 7 o'clock in the morning, where they enjoyed a plentiful breakfast consisting of salamis, ham, beer, wine, black coffee, mandarins and bananas. Probably, it was yet another moment when the physicians could forget for a few minutes that they were in the bombarded North Korean capital during the Korean War.[10)]

During wintertime, the Hungarian physicians were accommodated in local Korean peasant houses with the traditional *ondol* heating system. As mentioned above, in the case of those buildings, the smoke from the kitchen flowed through pipes under the floor of the rooms. However, the aforementioned plastic surgeon, Dr. Zoltán, wrote in his reminiscence that on one occasion, carbon monoxide leaked through the floor and the Hungarians who were sleeping in the rooms suffered minor smoke inhalation. The patients had to rest for a whole day and drink a great amount of strong coffee against the headache.[11)] Around the end of the year 1951, the Hungarian hospital and its staff celebrated not only Christmas and New Year's Eve, but also the birthday of Stalin on December 21 just like every country of the Soviet bloc at that time. On Stalin's birthday, the Korean staff received rewards for their diligence while the Hungarian physicians received a monthly quantity of cigarettes, soaps and tooth paste in advance. They spent Christmas together with the Hungarian diplomats at the hospital. The envoy and his colleagues arrived by their new truck and brought a couple of boxes of beer and figs. The envoy also delivered the Christmas presents which were sent by the relatives from Budapest. On New Year's Eve, the physicians visited the legation where a whole pig was prepared for dinner. The pig was previously brought from Shinuiju. However, on the way back the

10) Reminiscences of János Dénes, 51.

11) Zoltán, *Add vissza az arcomat*, 75.

Dr. János Zoltán, Hungarian plastic surgeon
(Semmelweis Medical History Museum, Budapest)

truck was attacked by an aircraft. Fortunately, the pig survived the attack and reached its destination at the legation, where the pig meat was enjoyed not only by the Hungarian diplomats and physicians, but also by the staff of the Polish and Czechoslovakian diplomatic missions.[12)]

The mission of the second group of the Hungarian physicians was completed in January 1952. Its members including Dr. Dénes received North Korean state awards. Before going back to Hungary, they gave Swiss-made Longines wristwatches to the Korean leadership of the hospital: to the director, to his deputy, to the political leader and to the caretaker of the hospital building. All of the other staff members received smaller gifts. Finally, the second group departed from Mangyongdae for Shinuiju on the board of three trucks and a Soviet-made Pobeda passenger car which was used by the females. The group left the territory of the DPRK on January 27, 1952. In his reminiscence, Dr. Dénes

12) Reminiscences of János Dénes, 54.

explained their journey back to Central Europe in details and mentioned that he made some observations about the characteristics of the Soviet Union. The first was about the Trans-Siberian railway; when the train stopped somewhere in the endless prairie, the buffet car was always sieged by the local residents who wanted to buy beer which was not available in their local shops. The second observation was about the circumstances in Moscow; the physicians visited some grocery stores which looked neat and nice from outside, but inside it was shocking due to the lack of goods. Furthermore, while shopping, some of the physicians lost their wallets which were probably stolen. The third observation was also made in Moscow where the physicians were invited to the flat of a Hungarian diplomat who showed them his television. Back in 1952, it was unimaginable for the ordinary people to have that kind of device.[13)]

---

13) Reminiscences of János Dénes, 57, 62.

X. High-ranking visitors and famous patients in the Hungarian hospital

According to a diplomatic report sent by the Hungarian legation in Pyongyang to Budapest in 1951, out of 32 North Korean hospitals only 10 had X-ray equipment, only 18 had a microscope, and only 17 had an operating table.[1] During the Korean War, the Hungarian hospital was one of the most well-equipped medical institutions in North Korea. Therefore, not only the younger brother and the uncle of Kim Il-sung but also various high-ranking officials, artists and intellectuals were treated there.[2] One of them was the forgotten Korean poet, Seol Chung-sik who moved to the North during the first phase of the Korean War. However, he suffered a heart attack in late October 1950, and he was treated in the Hungarian hospital in Manchuria in December 1950.[3] During his two-month-long recovery, he wrote a poem to his Hungarian doctors under the title of *Ujeongui seosasi* (The Epos of Friendship). According to the

1) Report written on July 24, 1951, by the Hungarian envoy Károly Pásztor. MNL XIX-J-14 box no. 1. 1-59.

2) Report written on October 20, 1951, by the Hungarian envoy Károly Pásztor. MNL XIX-J-1-k box no. 12. 28/c.

3) Seol Chung-sik (1912-1953): Korean poet. He studied in America in the late 1930s, became familiar with the Western literature and translated Shakespeare's works into Korean. During the second half of the 1940s, he worked as the editor of *The Seoul Times*. However, the English-language newspaper was closed due to political reasons. After moving to North Korea and having recovered from his illness with which he had been treated in the Hungarian hospital, he served as the Korean-English interpreter of the North Korean side during the armistice negotiations. However, as a Korean communist who came from the South, the poet was purged and executed in 1953.

Seol Chung-sik, Korean poet
(Public domain)

Hungarian correspondent Tibor Méray, the first version of the poem was translated into German by the aforementioned deputy director of the hospital, Major Hwang Su-bong. From the German translation, the physicians prepared a Hungarian version, but it was not published. However, a year later, Seol Chung-sik made an English translation with the assistance of two native English journalists – Allan Winnington and Wilfred Burchett – in Kaesong during the armistice negotiations, and then it was translated to Hungarian by a professional translator. Finally, the poem was successfully published in Budapest in 1952.

Another famous patient in the Hungarian hospital was actor Hwang Chul, who started his career during the Japanese rule, but after the liberation, he joined the communists and decided to move to the North.[4] He became actor at the DPRK's National Theater,

[4] Hwang Chul (1912-1961): Korean actor. He was born in South Chungchong Province and served as a taxi driver when he was young. He started his career as a trouper and became famous in Seoul, where he became the director of the Arang theater. In 1940, their play about the 19th century politician Kim Ok-kyun achieved great success, and Hwang became very

Hwang Chul, Korean actor
(Public domain)

and after the outbreak of the Korean War, he was assigned to a military unit for cultural support. Hwang Chul's unit moved to the direction of the front line, but on the way from Suwon to Pyongthaek, they were attacked by some American bombers. The actor was severely wounded and transferred to the Hungarian hospital where his right hand was amputated. During his recovery, he was interviewed by the aforementioned Hungarian correspondent, Tibor Méray who wrote a propagandistic short novel about the actor.[5] According to the heroic novel, the actor's unit saw a convoy of North Korean trucks during a night near Taejon. The trucks towed

popular. However, he had some unclarified affairs in his private life, and after the outbreak of the Pacific War, his troupe cooperated with the Japanese colonial authorities very actively. Therefore, Hwang's name can be found on the South Korean list of the pro-Japanese persons. After the liberation, the Arang theater ceased operation. Hwang had financial problems and heard circulating rumors stating that the circumstances for the actors were much better in the Northern half of the peninsula. In August 1948, he left for the North with his lover, Moon Jeong-bok. It is interesting to mention that Moon's son, Yang Thaek-cho, stayed in the South and also became a famous actor.

5) Méray, *Koreai jelentés*, 138-148.

four huge cannons and because of the noise of the engines, the drivers did not notice the sudden American bombardment. Hwang Chul wanted to warn the drivers to turn off the headlights, so he ran ahead to the trucks. However, an explosion wounded him.[6] It is interesting to mention that Hwang Chul later received a hand prosthesis made in Hungary and according to a diplomatic report, the famous historian Han Heung-su started to write a historical drama for the half-handed actor.[7] It is not clear if the drama was completed or not, but in 1953, the actor had the opportunity to play the role of the national hero Admiral Yi Sun-shin on the stage.[8]

In the second year of the Korean War, several important visitors and patients spent more or less time in the Hungarian hospital. On October 8, 1951, foreign minister Park Hon-yong and health minister Yi Byeong-nam visited the physicians in Oru-ri, 5 kilometers away from Mangyongdae. According to the sources, the ministers were satisfied with what they saw despite a huge air attack taking place around the village. After the attack, the ministers were given some snacks which were served on the bank of the neighboring stream.[9] A few days later, on October 14, the North Korean artist ensemble gave a performance to the Hungarian physicians. The iconic leader of the ensemble was the legendary

---

6) Méray, *Koreai jelentés*, 138-148.

7) Report written on June 7, 1952, by the Hungarian envoy Károly Pásztor. MNL XIX-J-1-k box no. 12. 28/c.

8) Yi Sun-shin (1545–1598): admiral, national hero of the Imjin War. He was born in Hanseong (present-day Seoul), passed his military examinations and gained experience in the defence against the Jurchens at the northern border. In the begining of the Japanese invasion against Korea, he was the commander of the Left Jeolla Naval District and led the glorious victory at Hansan Island; the battle was called 'Salamis of Korea'. It is interesting to mention that Yi Sun-shin's cult emerged in Central and Eastern Europe during the Korean War in the early 1950s, and a parallel was drawn between the Korean fights against the Japanese in the 16th century and the North Korean fights against the Americans in the Korean War. In Hungary, it was correspondent Tibor Méray who first mentioned the Korean national hero in his articles and books.

9) Zoltán, *Add vissza az arcomat*, 119-120.

Foreign minister Park Hon-yong visiting the houses of the hospital in Oru-ri, the neighborhood of Mangyongdae
(Photo Archive of the Hungarian Ministry of Defense, Budapest)

Korean dancer, Choi Seung-hee (1911-1969) who moved her dance academy to Beijing during the war. Her husband, the communist intellectual Ahn Mak (1910-1959), was operated in the Hungarian hospital by Dr. Dénes in November 1951 after he was injured severely. According to Dr. Dénes, he was shot in the head, but there is no information as to how it happened or if it had anything to do with his purge and execution later. Dr. Dénes only mentioned that

Foreign minister Park Hon-yong in the hospital in Mangyongdae. The second person from the left is Károly Práth, the Hungarian envoy to the DPRK
(Photo Archive of the Hungarian Ministry of Defense, Budapest)

Ahn's condition improved a lot after the surgery.[10)]

Turning back to the high-ranking visitors in the Hungarian hospital, it was expected that on December 12, 1951, Kim Il-sung would visit the institution personally to give medals to the Hungarian doctors. However, the leader did not appear and in the evening, the physicians were taken to the Moranbong Hill where, in the bunker deep under the hill, a large-scale dance performance was given by the pupils of Choi Seung-hee. Kim Il-sung also attended the event, but the medals were not presented. The awards were transferred to them later, right before the second group of the Hungarian medical team left on January 29, 1952. Since Kim Il-sung did not attend personally, the medals were given to them by the North Korean health minister.[11)] In the spring of 1952, the

10) Reminiscences of János Dénes, 52.
11) Reminiscences of János Dénes, 52, 56.

Ahn Mak, Korean communist intellectual
(Public domain)

Yim Hwa, Korean poet
(Public domain)

famous Korean poet, Yim Hwa (1908-1953), was also hospitalized in the Hungarian hospital. According to an archive diplomatic report, his condition was critical, but his life was saved. The report does not go into details regarding how he was injured or what happened exactly, but there are some hints suggesting that it was something 'very serious', which could even have been a suicide attempt.[12] According to the report of the Hungarian envoy Károly Pásztor, the May Day celebration was held at the Hungarian hospital in company with some leading North Korean intellectuals in 1952. Along with the aforementioned Yim Hwa, Kim Kwi-ryon, a poetess and Kim Soon-nam, a composer, participated in the event.[13]

12) Report written on June 11, 1952, by the Hungarian envoy Károly Pásztor. MNL XIX-J-1-k box no. 12. 28/c.

13) Kim Soon-nam (1917–1983 or 1986): Korean composer. He was born in Seoul and studied music in Tokyo from 1938. In the year of the national liberation, he joined the bustling cultural life in Seoul. However, due to the chaotic circumstances and the food shortage in the provinces, he became disillusioned soon. One of his composition was the *Inmin Hangjaengga* (Song of the People's Resistance) whose lyric was written by Yim Hwa.

Major Hwang Su-bong (on the left), the deputy director of the Hungarian hospital
(Semmelweis Medical History Museum, Budapest)

Károly Pásztor wrote that the 'greatest composer' of Korea was introduced to him by Major Hwang Su-bong, the North Korean deputy director of the hospital, who himself was also an amateur musician, good pianist as well as talented singer. Kim Soon-nam had a lot of plans for cultural exchange between North Korea and Hungary.[14] As it was written in the summary report by the envoy, Károly Pásztor, the Hungarian movie, Déryné ('Mrs. Déry') was screened during the May Day celebration for the participants who were welcomed not only by the envoy and Dr. Ri Kang-guk but also by the aunt of Kim Il-sung who was still living in Mangyongdae at that time.[15]

Kim Soon-nam moved to the North in 1948, where he became the director of the composition department at the Pyongyang National Music School. He was purged during the internal campaign against the communists who came from the South.

14) Report written on May 28, 1952, by the Hungarian envoy Károly Pásztor. MNL XIX-J-1-k-1945–1964-Korea box no. 9. 18/c.

Kim Soon-nam, Korean composer
(National Archives of Hungary, Ministry of Foreign Affairs' Directory)

As mentioned above, the vast majority of the North Korean elite was purged sooner or later. Therefore, the Hungarian physicians could not avoid witnessing the internal turbulences. In August 1953, during the regime's first large-scale show trial which targeted the cadres who came from the Southern part of the

15) Report written on June 7, 1952, by the Hungarian envoy Károly Pásztor. MNL XIX-J-1-k box no. 12. 28/c.

The aunt of prime minister Kim Il-sung on the May Day event at the Hungarian hospital
(Photo Archive of the Hungarian Ministry of Defense, Budapest)

peninsula, foreign minister Park Hon-yong was purged, and poet Yim Hwa who had once been taken to the Hungarian hospital in critical condition was also executed. The other poet, Seol Chung-sik whose epos was published in Budapest, was also accused of being an American spy. The Hungarian readers were probably shocked when they saw the news about the poet's execution in the leading newspapers.[16)] The Korean director of the Hungarian hospital, the aforementioned Dr. Ri, was also accused of being an American spy. The Hungarian envoy wrote in his report that the official explanation stated that after the success of the 'conspiration', Park Hon-yong would have been the new prime minister, and Dr. Ri would have been the new foreign minister.[17)] The Hungarian physicians were shocked at the news about the

16) "Államellenes kém- és terrorközpont pere..." (Trial of a spy and terrorist group – in Hungarian) *Szabad Nép*, August 9, 1953.

17) Report written on August 8, 1953, by the Hungarian envoy Károly Pásztor. MNL XIX-J-1-k-1945–1964-Korea box no. 12. 30/c.

execution of the former director. They also heard that the deputy director, the aforementioned Major Hwang Su-bong, was also arrested soon after. However, the outcome of his trial remained unknown to the Hungarians.[18] Composer Kim Soon-nam was purged, too; he lost all of his official posts and then transferred to the shipyard of Sinpho in South Hamgyong Province. In the factory, he was responsible for thawing the resin. The exact place and time of his death is still unknown.

In April 1956, the names of the North Korean officials and intellectuals who had been purged at the end of the Korean War appeared once more in a Hungarian diplomatic report. According to the document, Moon Jae-soo, North Korean chargé d'affaires to Budapest, visited the Hungarian Ministry of Foreign Affairs and asked the Hungarian officials to give back all of the North Korean newsreels which were taken before 1955. The goal of the request was probably to remove traces of Park Hon-yong, the purged foreign minister, from the newsreels. The diplomat also asked the Hungarian officials to stop translating the works of some North Korean intellectuals and to recall the translated books and works that were already distributed to the bookstores and libraries. Poet Seol Chung-sik, Poet Yim Hwa and Composer Kim Soon-nam who were the former patients and visitors of the Hungarian hospital were among the North Korean intellecturals.[19]

Around the end of the decade, the communist intellectual Ahn Mak who was operated in the Hungarian hospital, was also purged and executed due to the actual turbulences in the North Korean regime. His wife, the legendary dancer Choi Seung-hee, was purged in the 1960s, but the circumstances of her death

---

18) Zoltán, *Add vissza az arcomat*, 102-103, 105.

19) Report written by the Far Eastern Department of the Hungarian Ministry of Foreign Affairs in April 17, 1956. MNL XIX-J-1-k-1945- 1964-Korea box no. 9. 18/d.

remained unknown. As István Garajszki, a retired Hungarian diplomat, shared it with the author of this book, her downfall happened after an incident of which the members of the diplomatic corps in Pyongyang at that time also heard. According to the rumor, Kim Il-sung wanted to congratulate Choi Seung-hee after one of her performances, and he entered her dressing room. However, she received the leader disrespectfully.[20)]

[20)] The author's conversation with István Garajszki. (Budapest, February 6, 2017.)

XI. From Mangyongdae to Huichon

The third group of the Hungarian medical teams left Budapest at the end of December 1951. One of its members, Mária Nagy, wrote in her reminiscence that the weather was frosty when they crossed the Amnok (Yalu) River from Andong to Shinuiju. A huge number of North Korean people were waiting for them outside waving flags to welcome the Hungarians despite the cold.[1] The group arrived at Mangyongdae on January 18, 1952, and it seems, from the official record on their activities, the group paid particular attention to the protocol duties. The newcomers went straight to visit the house of Kim Il-sung's family and met his relatives who were still living there. Moreover, on April 15, 1952, the birthday of the North Korean leader, the Hungarian physicians mounted a memorial plaque on the wall of the house to show their respect.

Meanwhile, the North Korean military held an award ceremony in the Hungarian hospital. According to the official record, two of the Korean leaders of the institute, director Dr. Ri Kang-guk and deputy director Hwang Su-bong, were decorated during the event.[2] As it was mentioned above, one and a half years after the ceremony, both of them were purged. The aforementioned plastic surgeon, Dr. János Zoltán, described one very touching moment in his reminiscence. One day before his departure back to

---

1) Letter written probably in 1986 by the Hungarian paramedic Mária Nagy. HM HIM MN Kgy: C-223

2) Report written probably in late 1952 by the Hungarian physicians Dr. János Bonta and Dr. György Bálint. HM HIM MN Kgy: C-226

A Street in Pyongyang. The picture was probably taken by a member of the Hungarian medical team in 1952
(Photo Archive of the Hungarian Ministry of Defense, Budapest)

Hungary, Dr. Zoltán was summoned by the deputy director, Hwang Su-bong, to the hall of the hospital where the director, Dr. Ri Kang-guk, was already waiting for them behind the table. In front of him were 50-60 North Korean soldiers who recovered from injuries sitting on the floor. Hwang asked the surgeon to sit down on one of the chairs behind the table, and then he started to speak to the soldiers. According to Dr. Zoltán, it was a long speech in Korean language which the surgeon hardly understood. However, he noticed soon that the eyes of the soldiers were filled with tears and he slowly came to understand that the young men who saw numerous deaths in the battlefield were crying because their physician from Europe would leave the country soon.[3)]

---

3) Zoltán, *Add vissza az arcomat*, 118-119.

A destroyed district in Pyongyang. The picture was probably taken by a member of the Hungarian medical team in 1952
(Photo Archive of the Hungarian Ministry of Defense, Budapest)

The social activities in Pyongyang were held in the underground theater at Moranbong Hill. According to the official record, the leadership of the Hungarian hospital visited the theater on various occasions: May Day reception where they could meet with Kim Il-sung personally, International Children's Day event on May 31, the celebration of the second anniversary of the outbreak of the Korean War on June 25, Polish National Day reception on July 22 and Chinese National Day reception on August 1. On the occasion of the anniversary of the Korean liberation from the Japanese colonial rule on August 12, the leadership of the Hungarian hospital was invited to the reception where they had an opportunity again to meet with Kim Il-sung and Park Jong-ae. On August 20, the Hungarian legation held the National Day celebration at the theater where the Romanians also held their own reception three

The decorative gate of the 'Second Unit' of the Hungarian hospital in a village around Mangyongdae
(Photo Archive of the Hungarian Ministry of Defense, Budapest)

days later.[4)]

In addition to the social events, the third group of the Hungarian medical teams organized the hospital's first conference on medical science on the weekend of July 26 and 27, 1952. The Hungarian doctors invited their Central and Eastern European colleagues to the event. The Czechoslovakians and the Romanians participated in the conference while the Bulgarians did not due to the long distance between their institute and the Hungarian hospital. Although the Soviets agreed to participate, they never showed up. According to the summary report on the conference, the event started a bit later than scheduled on Saturday morning. The guests

4) The National Day of Hungary on August 20 stands for the establishment of the first-ever Hungarian state by King Saint Stephen I. However, during the communism, the National Day was referred as the 'Day of the Constitution'. The Romanian National Day was a commemoration on the country's turn from the Axes to the Allies which happened in 1944.

The decorative gate of the 'Third Unit' of the Hungarian hospital in a village around Mangyongdae
(Photo Archive of the Hungarian Ministry of Defense, Budapest)

were greeted by director Dr. Ri Kang-guk whose words were interpreted to German and Russian. After the Hungarian envoy gave a short speech, a lecture about the activities of the third Hungarian group was held. Finally, the participants saw a photo exhibition prepared by the Hungarian legation. The luncheon was between 2 and 4 p.m., followed by the first section of the conference at 4 o'clock. According to the program book of the event which was printed in Korean and Russian, the organizers wanted to screen the Hungarian movie 'Déryné' ('Mrs. Déry') from 9 o'clock for the participants, but they could not make it due to the electricity shortage in the evening.[5] The conference resumed next morning. For the closing ceremony, Korean artists held a concert for the participants. The Hungarian envoy wrote in his report that the

---

5) Report written on August 11, 1952, by diplomat Béla Hegedűs. MNL XIX-J-1-k box no. 12. 28/c.

conference was very successful, which made the Romanian physicians announce that they would like to organize a similar event soon.[6)]

Meanwhile, the reputation of the Hungarian hospital was spread to the other side of the frontline. According to the reminiscences of the abovementioned plastic surgeon, Dr. János Zoltán, South Korean soldiers crossed the frontline from time to time to have their injuries treated at the Hungarian hospital.[7)] This information was also confirmed by another physician, Dr. János Bonta who served as a radiologist of the third medical group in 1952. According to Dr. Bonta, on one occasion, the hospital was inspected by the North Korean state securities, and twelve South Korean soldiers were found and deported from the wards.[8)] The summary report also mentioned that the bombardment against the hospital also killed South Korean soldiers who 'were working'at the hospital. However, it is not clear whether the South Koreans were deserters or prisoners of the war.[9)]

Speaking of the third group of the Hungarian medical teams, from the early summer of 1952, the physicians did various sports activities in their free time even during the war. As did the members of the previous group, they swam in the Taedong River and played football or handball with the Korean staff. However, they were never able to forget the fact that they were in the middle of the battlefield of the Korean War because bomb blast hit the Hungarian hospital at least four times in that year: on May 24, June 2, June 6 and October 31, followed by several smaller attacks. Amid these

---

6) Report written on August 11, 1952, by envoy Károly Pásztor. MNL XIX-J-1-k box no. 12. 28/c.

7) Zoltán, *Add vissza az arcomat*, 73.

8) Bihari, Tamás: "Elfelejtett internacionalisták" (Forgotten internacionalists – in Hungarian) *A Világ*, January 11, 1990.

9) Report written on November 22, 1952, by the Hungarian charge d'affaires Józsefné Turai. MNL XIX-J-1-k box no. 12. 28/c.

attacks in August, an oral surgeon, Dr. Zoltán Frankl (1907-1998), got seriously injured and was sent back to Hungary on September 8. According to his reminiscences, he arrived in North Korea after undergoing personal traumas caused by his Jewish background. His parents were killed during the WW2 while Dr. Frankl was taken to the concentration camp of Mauthausen.[10] The holocaust survivor physician wrote that he was really distressed in North Korea not only by the despotic political leader of the third group but also by the bomb attack he had just survived from. According to his reminiscences, one day in August, despite the intensive traffic in the air, he left Mangyongdae to examine his patients in Nam-ri. Dr. Frankl received fourteen patients. However, due to the increasing numbers of the air attacks, he left Nam-ri for Mangyongdae where he had departed. On the way back, he found a shelter where some Korean cadres of the hospital hid themselves. Dr. Frankl was sitting in the shelter with them when there was a huge explosion. The physician was buried in the ground but pulled out immediately by the Koreans. Due to his bad physical condition, the doctor was quickly brought to Mangyongdae. After his repatriation to Hungary, Minister of Health Affairs visited him at the hospital in Budapest and asked the doctor to file a false report that he was injured in a car accident, not in the bombardment. It is assumed that the high level cadres were concerned that the Hungarian doctors would no longer join the next groups heading for Korea if they were aware of how dangerous the mission was. Dr. Frankl refused the request, which later worked against him. When the other doctors received the Hungarian state awards for their service in North Korea, Dr. Frankl received only the lowest level of acknowledgment. Moreover, when a photo board was made for the third group, the editor did not include his picture in the board leaving his place

10) Letter written in March 1, 1984, by the Hungarian physician Dr. Zoltán Frankl. HM HIM MN Kgy: C-223

blank.[11] Dr. Frankl also had difficult times during the anti-communist Hungarian revolution in 1956 when he treated the injuries day and night in the Péterfi hospital in Budapest. After all, the oral surgeon decided to leave Hungary and continue his profession in England where he became succesful and established.

The fourth group of the Hungarian medical teams arrived in the DPRK on September 26, 1952. One of its members, Dr. Antal Nádasi, wrote in his reminiscences that their first experience in Korea was witnessing the destroyed city of Shinuiju while they were cutting cross by trucks under the gloomy weather. They saw the ruins of Pyongyang. However, when arriving at Mangyongdae, all of them were surprised at the fully intact buildings of the Hungarian hospital. Nevertheless, only one month after their arrival, the fourth group experienced one of the biggest-ever bombardment against the hospital. Dr. Nádasi wrote that at 4:30 in the morning of October 31, 1952, loud noises woke them up. They thought it was a thunderstorm outside and they felt that the hill under the hospital was shaking. One of the physicians tried to light a cigarette but all the others warned him to stop it immediately. At first, the physicians hid themselves under the beds, then moved to a shelter. According to Dr. Nádasi, many of the patients and the local staff died during the bombardment.[12] This was also confirmed by the summary report of the Hungarian legation. According to the report, 16 people were dead and 37 were injured during the bombardment. Three of the casualties were civilians and four were South Korean soldiers. The extent of their injuries was not described in the report. Among the victims was a female teacher of the Kim Il-sung Elementary School in Budapest. The institution

---

11) Letter written in March 1, 1984, by the Hungarian physician Dr. Zoltán Frankl. HM HIM MN Kgy: C-223

12) Letter written probably in 1986 by the Hungarian physician Dr. Antal Nádasi. HM HIM MN Kgy: C-223

was established in the Hungarian capital at the end of 1951 for the North Korean orphans and school children who were studying in the Central European country. The female teacher who also served as the director of the aforementioned school visited the Hungarian hospital to see her husband who was hospitalized.[13] According to the archive document, the first director of the Kim Il-sung Elementary School was Kim Wol-ok who was assumed as the victim of the bombardment.[14]

The summary report also mentioned that two Hungarian citizens were injured during the attack: a man fell down while he was running to the shelter and later sent back to Hungary due to the post-traumatic stress; and a woman had her leg injured.[15] Dr. Nádasi recalled that, since the bombardment on October 31, the everyday life in the Hungarian hospital had changed. The doctors lived in the shelter for a few days, then moved to the nearest wooden houses from the shelter.[16] Meanwhile, the Hungarians were warned by the North Korean military commanders that hostile spy activities were likely to be detected in the territory of the hospital. Allegedly, one of the arrested spies admitted that he gave light signals to the attacking aircrafts on October 31.[17] Probably, the fear from the hostile activities was the reason why each and every staff member of the Hungarian hospital was given a pistol.[18]

---

13) Report written on November 22, 1952, by the Hungarian charge d'affaires Józsefné Turai. MNL XIX-J-1-k box no. 12. 28/c.

14) Chomeo, Mose (Csoma, Mózes): *Honggari choichoui hangukhak hakja bukhaneul mannada.* (The first-ever Hungarian Koreanist scholar meets North Korea – in Korean) Seoul: Nosvos, 2015, 38.

15) Report written on November 22, 1952, by the Hungarian charge d'affaires Józsefné Turai. MNL XIX-J-1-k box no. 12. 28/c.

16) Letter written probably in 1986 by the Hungarian physician Dr. Antal Nádasi. HM HIM MN Kgy: C-223

17) Report written about the developments in the Hungarian hospital between November 1, 1952, and January 20, 1953. HIM MN Kgy: C-226

18) Letter written in November 1986, by the Hungarian X-ray technician László Gera. HM HIM MN Kgy: C-223

The Hungarian physicians leaving Mangyongdae in March 1953
(Semmelweis Medical History Museum, Budapest)

Dr. Antal Nádasi wrote in his reminiscences that the atmosphere of the Hungarian hospital became tense from January 1953. One night, loud shouts were heard in the neighborhood, and somebody fired his pistol; hence, the Hungarians assumed that their hospital would be evacuated and moved to somewhere else soon. In February, a great number of 'Chinese People's Volunteers' arrived in the neighborhood and the rumor that the Americans would land near the hospital soon spread.[19] Finally, the North Korean authorities decided to move the Hungarian hospital to a much safer location in March 1953. It was in the neighborhood of Huichon city, 166 kilometers north from Pyongyang. The former building in Mangyongdae was handed over to the 'Chinese People's Volunteers' who continued to use it as a hospital building.

Moving to the new location was described by Dr. Antal Nádasi in details. At the end of March, two or three trucks transported pieces of equipment and medicines from Mangyongdae

19) Letter written probably in 1986 by the Hungarian physician Dr. Antal Nádasi. HM HIM MN Kgy: C-223

to Huichon every day. Each physician got in each truck and moved to the new place. Dr. Nádasi wrote that while he was in the truck running in the outskirt of Pyongyang, he observed that Chinese checkpoints were installed on the highways in every 2-3 kilometers. The Chinese soldiers warned people for the air raids by waving their flags during the daytime and by shooting rifles during the night. Dr. Nádasi's truck reached the Chongchon River at dawn. After seeing the ruins of Huichon, the truck followed the sinuous path through the trees of the mountain.[20] According to the reminiscence of Dr. Nádasi, the barracks of the new hospital were built on the floodplain of the tributary of a river, but its exact location is not specified. There are two rivers in the region: one is the aforementioned Chongchon River and the other is the Huichon River. One of the sources wrote only about the Chongchon River while the other wrote only about the Huichon River. It is clear that the hospital was not located at a single location, but it was separated into multiple bodies by using peasant houses lined along 12 kilometers of the bank of the 'river'.[21] Moving the whole institutes took 10 days until the last truck arrived in the neighborhood of Huichon on April 2, 1953.[22]

The fifth group of the Hungarian medical teams departed from Budapest on June 1, 1953. One of its members was a 27-year-old young physician, Dr. Ödön Sátori who wrote a very interesting reminiscence about his observation. Before their departure, the Headquarter of the Hungarian Working People's

---

20) The Chongchon River is the same with the ancient Salsu River, where the famous medieval battle happened between Goguryeo and the Sui Empire in 612.

21) Dr. Frigyes Kulka, a member of the fifth group of the Hungarian medical teams, mentioned only the Chongchon River in his reminiscence. Source: *A Jalu-folyótól a 38. szélességi fokig*. (From the Yalu River to the 38th parallel – Text of a radio interview with Dr. Frigyes Kulka, written in 1956), 5.

22) Letter written probably in 1986 by the Hungarian physician Dr. Antal Nádasi. HM HIM MN Kgy: C-223

Welcome rally for the fifth group of the Hungarian physicians at the border town of Shinuiju
(From the heritage of Dr. Ödön Sátori)

Party organized a generous farewell reception for the doctors on the Margaret island which is one of the most picturesque parts of Budapest. The group left for East Asia by train and reached the Soviet-Chinese border in Manzhouli from where a Western-made express train carried them to Mukden. Dr. Sátori mentioned that the last wagon of the train was an observation car to enjoy the outside views during the journey. The train also had an office room for the high level Chinese officials which was an unthinkable luxury for the Hungarians at that time. From Mukden, the medical team continued the journey on an ordinary passanger train on which Chinese soldiers were also heading for North Korea. All of them carried machine guns, but the Hungarians were surprised not only at the guns, but at the lack of military rank marking on their uniforms.[23)]

---

23) Sátori, Ödön: *Koreai emlékeim I.* (My Korean memories 1 – manuscipt in Hungarian), 2-4. Archive of the Semmelweis Medical History Museum (Hungary, Budapest)

Dr. Ödön Sátori, Hungarian physician
(Semmelweis Medical History Museum, Budapest)

In the Chinese border city of Andong, the team had a long and unpleasant discussion with the custom officials because the doctors carried 1,5 kilogramms of poppy seeds with them for their colleagues. The seeds were the main ingredients of a Hungarian traditional food. After solving the problems, the medical team crossed the Amnok (Yalu) River by truck. Dr. Sátori wrote that his first experience in North Korea was massive air attacks; the American aircrafts bombed the bridges of the river and the anti-aircraft guns fired into the sky with loud growls. In Shinuiju, a great number of local people welcomed the medical team waving Hungarian and North Korean flags and singing the national anthems along with a series of 'fireworks' of the anti-aircraft guns. The young Hungarian physician emphasized that, during the journey, whenever they passed through the villages, the Korean residents always raised their thumbs up at the foreign doctors to show their friendship. When the medical team was attacked by two warplanes in the valley, a huge anti-aircraft fire suddenly emerged

The Huichon River
(From the heritage of Dr. Ödön Sátori)

from the neighboring hills, where Chinese soldiers were ambushed. It is very interesting to compare these experiences with what the first Hungarian medical team had two years earlier when real air defence did not even exist in North Korea.[24)]

Finally, the fifth group arrived at the valley of the Huichon River where the hospital was located. The hospital used small peasant houses and excavated holes for patient's rooms. According to Dr. Sátori, the members of the fourth team who greeted them were very tanned and wore North Korean military unifroms without rank markings. The old members prepared for various Hungarian-traditional dishes for the newcomers; they bought a pig from a Korean peasant for the feast. The Hungarian envoy to North Korea, Károly Pásztor, attended the very first meeting with the newcomers. According to Dr. Sátori, the diplomat warned the young physician and his fellows that all kinds of intimate relations with Korean girls were strictly forbidden.[25)] However, even before building up any

24) Sátori, *Koreai emlékeim I*, 5.

Temporary bridge over the Huichon River. The one in front is Dr. Ödön Sátori.
(From the heritage of Dr. Ödön Sátori)

Korean women are washing clothes in the river. In the middle is Dr. Ödön Sátori.
(From the heritage of Dr. Ödön Sátori)

25) Sátori, *Koreai emlékeim I*, 10.

intimate relations, what the newcomers met with was the first air attack against the hospital. Dr. Sátori wrote that he heard whizzing sounds during the surgery when the aircrafts were circling around over the hospital followed by a huge explosion. The window glasses scattered and the physician was going to halt the operation. However, his assistant, a 17-year-old Korean nurse, stayed calm and asked him in Korean: 'Moya? Hango issumnikka?' (What happend? Was it an air raid?) Hearing her calm voice, Dr. Sátori was able to calm himself down as well and decided to stay and finish the surgery in the operation room.[26)]

In the summer of 1953, during the monsoon season, the level of the river rose. Once, one of their cars got stuck in the overflowing river. They tried to pull out the vehicle using their Hungarian-made Csepel truck. Three Chinese soldiers and a North Korean captain tried to help them until they were swept away by the water. Their bodies have yet to be found.[27)] Ilona Kormos, a nurse of the fifth group, had a similar experience. When her truck got stuck in the river, the Hungarian driver was able to get out and swim to the riverbank while two North Korean soldiers were still struggling to escape from the vehicle which turned on its side. It was impossible to take them out in the dark, but the people on the bank lit a fire and kept speaking to the soldiers all night. The next morning, a Korean major came to rescue them riding a cow. Unfortunately, in the rescuing process, the major was swept away by the river and gone missing. It is not clear from the reminiscenes whether or not the two soldiers who got into trouble the day before survived. It is assumed that they did because the symbolic mourning ceremony held by the Koreans was only for the missing major. Ilona Kormos also wrote about another incident. When the

---

26) Sátori, *Koreai emlékeim I*, 11.

27) Sátori, Ödön: *Koreai emlékeim II*. (My Korean memories 2 – manuscipt in Hungarian), 1.

Ilona Kormos, Hungarian nurse
(Semmelweis Medical History Museum, Budapest)

Hungarian physicians were invited by the Czechoslovakian medical team to their hospital, they had to cross the overflowing river to get to the hospital and their jeep got stuck in the river. In the vehicle were five people in their formal dresses which got soaked immediately. Fortunately, Chinese soldiers showed up on the riverbank and helped them to pull out the jeep. On the way to the Czechoslovakian hospital, all the Hungarian males and females took off their clothes to dry them in the headwind.[28]

Ilona Kormos also wrote a less tragic episode about her stay in Huichon. She and her colleages crossed the temporary bridge of the river to go to the neighbouring village. In the evening, the bridge was destroyed by the river. Fortunately, some Korean soldiers helped them to move to the other side safely. She wrote that the Hungarian nurses could easily mingle with the local people. According to her letter, the local peasants often invited them to their

28) Letter written in November 23, 1986, by the Hungarian nurse, Ilona Kormos. HM HIM MN Kgy: C-223

A fallen empty fuel tank of an aircraft in the courtyard of the house used by the Hungarian doctors
(From the collection of Dr. Janina Kulka)

Dr. Frigyes Kulka and the shower made with the fallen fuel tank of an aircraft
(From the collection of Dr. Janina Kulka)

houses and offered them boiled potatos, corns and cigarettes.[29] The aforementioned physician, Dr. Ödön Sátori, also wrote about an interesting episode in Huichon. The Hungarians found an empty fuel tank which fell from an American aircraft which they converted to a non-stop shower equipment. They made holes on the top of the oval metal tank, connected it to the river and had a refreshing shower for the hot summer time.[30]

29) Letter written in November 23, 1986, by the Hungarian nurse, Ilona Kormos. HM HIM MN Kgy: C-223

30) Sátori, *Koreai emlékeim II*, 1.

XII. The role of the Hungarian hospital after the armistice

As it was mentioned above, the fifth group of the Hungarian medical teams started its activities in the region of Huichon. According to the report of Dr. Béla Berényi, the leader of the group, the biggest difficulty was the decentralization of the hospital.[1] Each department was geographically separated from each other by river courses. During the monsoon season, the river overflowed, which caused the disconnection between the departments for days. The wards got soaked as the rainwater reached up to the height of the beds. The operating room was located in a peasant house where battery lamps were used due to the lack of electricity for the surgical procedure after the sunset. An autoclave machine operated by coal was used for disinfection, but the insufficient coal supply during the monsoon had one of the physicians modify the machine to be operated by wood.

Dr. Béla Berényi also wrote about a small conflict among the Hungarian physicians and the North Korean military commanders of the hospital. The North Koreans prohibited the Hungarians from providing the civilians with medicines. The military officials underlined that the hospital was a military institute while the Hungarians emphasized that the civilians should also be offered with medicines from the hospital as there were no other medical

---

1) Report written by Dr. Béla Berényi, the leader of the fifth group of the Hungarian medical teams. HM HIM MN Kgy: C-223

institutions in the region. Korean citizens were not aware of that medicines were prohibited to be shared by the Korean commanders but they thought that it was Hungarians who did not want to share any medicines with them. In the end, a compromise was made among the commanders that the medicines – except the Penicillin and Streptomycin – would be also given to the civilians. A report written by Dr. Berényi mentioned that the pharmacy of the hospital had been operated by an incompetent Korean paramedic for a long time. Not only was he incapable of managing the inventory, but gave false information to the patients about the stock of the necessary medicines; he told the patients the medicines on demand were out of stock several times although they were not.

After the armistice was signed on July 27, 1953, the atmosphere of the Hungarian hospital in Korea became much more peaceful. In the last days of August, four members from the hospital went to Pyongyang to attend the congress of surgeons. One of them was Dr. Frigyes Kulka, a well-known Hungarian pulmonologist.[2] Even though the physicians had to walk 35 kilometers in the heavy monsoon rain, crossed several flooded streams to reach the nearest train station, they safely arrived in Pyongyang. However, by mistake of the organizers, their lectures were not programmed in the congress except the presentation of their Korean colleague who escorted them to the venue. Speaking of the activities of the hospital under the peaceful circumstances, the Hungarian physicians initiated a screening test campaign for the local citizens in September 1953. At first, students of a neighboring school were screened for tuberculosis, then 240 workers from the truck factory of Huichon had their chests X-rayed.

After the armistice, the authorities of the DPRK decided to

---

2) His son, János Kulka (born in 1958), is a famous contemporary actor in Hungary.

Dr. Frigyes Kulka with two North Korean soldiers around Huichon
(From the collection of Dr. Janina Kulka)

Part of a railroad bridge around Huichon
(From the heritage of Dr. Ödön Sátori)

Shell of a destroyed locomotive around Huichon
(From the heritage of Dr. Ödön Sátori)

relocate the hospital to Sariwon city in North Hwanghae Province. However, the circumstances in Sariwon did not allow it to move yet. A provisional location was designated in Songrim for the Hungarian hospital. On October 16, 1953, six trucks were transporting the pieces of equipment of the hospital to the train station of Huichon, where some tents were set up while loading the freight train. Meanwhile, several members of the hospital, including the aforementioned Dr. Frigyes Kulka, departed for Songrim to prepare for the accommodation for the group. With the assistance of the local People's Committee, the forerunners successfully built a house equipped with a heating system. According to the reminiscences of the Hungarian pulmonologist Dr. Miklós Böszörményi in the sixth group, the main building of the hospital in Songrim was formerly used as a prison.[3] As the preparation for opening took

3) Letter written on November 1, 1986, by the Hungarian pulmonologist Dr. Miklós Böszörményi. HM HIM MN Kgy: C-305

The Hungarian flag flies on the hospital building in Songrim
(Semmelweis Medical History Museum, Budapest)

longer than expected, the members of the group left Huichon and went to the Hungarian legation in the neighborhood of Pyongyang on November 1, 1953. The legation was probably located in the valley of the Sopho Mountain at that time.[4] The physicians spent three days in the diplomatic inn enjoying the full service. The group could leave for Songrim on November 5 but their journey was not free from troubles. Unfortunately, their truck stopped on the way and the Hungarians had to walk at least 7 kilometers to reach the destination.[5]

According to the aforementioned nurse, Ilona Kormos, when they arrived at Songrim, the Hungarian national flag was already hoisted on the building. The physicians were welcomed

4) Email message sent on November 20, 2020, by the Russian Embassy in Pyongyang to the author.

5) Report written by Dr. Béla Berényi, the leader of the fifth group of the Hungarian medical teams. HM HIM MN Kgy: C-223

The hospital building in Songrim. A photo taken by Dr. Ödön Sátori
(From the heritage of Dr. Ödön Sátori)

The members of the fifth Hungarian group at the iron foundry in Songrim. The director of the foundry is in the middle and the third person from the right is Dr. Frigyes Kulka
(From the collection of Dr. Janina Kulka)

with 50 kilograms of bananas prepared by the director of the local iron foundry. It seems bananas could be found in North Korea during the postwar years. They were probably imported from China. The director of the foundry agreed with the Hungarians that his staff would wire all the rooms of the hospital for electricity and would produce iron beds for wards.[6)]

The reminiscences of the aforementioned Dr. Ödön Sátori also confirmed that the type of tasks of the physicians was completely changed in the new hospital. They had to take care of the epidemics and general illnesses instead of war injuries. At first, approximately 1,000 patients were waiting to see a doctor in front of the hospital. Although the physicians tried to examine them as fast as possible, a small child with a high fever died while waiting. In this period, the Hungarians observed various exotic diseases which they learned only from the classic medical book, *Tropical Diseases*, written by Patrick Manson in 1898. The patients came to the hospital from far-away regions as well. Sometimes their purpose of visit was irrational; according to Dr. Sátori, one of the patients asked the doctors to cure his baldness.[7)]

The sixth group of the Hungarian medical teams arrived in the DPRK on February 19, 1954. The new team was a lot larger than the previous ones; 47 people in total including the wives of the physicians who were allowed to accompany their husbands after the armistice. Pulmonologist Dr. Miklós Böszörményi wrote in his reminiscences that they were the first among the Hungarian groups, who traveled by train from the Sino-Korean border to Pyongyang.[8)] They saw bomb funnels along the railroad, the train stopped at destroyed towns and they observed the legacy of the war both in

---

6) Letter written in November 23, 1986, by the Hungarian nurse, Ilona Kormos. HM HIM MN Kgy: C-223

7) Sátori, *Koreai emlékeim II*, 5.

8) Letter written on November 1, 1986, by the Hungarian pulmonologist Dr. Miklós Böszörményi. HM HIM MN Kgy: C-305

Songrim and Sariwon where many people were still living in the holes on the ground. In the first half of 1954, the Hungarian hospital was operated in parallel in both locations. It is only assumed that they moved to Sariwon by the mid-year. The exact date of moving is still unknown. Only 10-15 house remained intact in Sariwon which used to have 50,000 citizens. The public transportation between the towns stopped operating, trucks and horse carriages were too rare to be found and the locals usually walked tens of kilometres to reach their destination. Dr. Böszörményi observed several times that homeless intellectual families carried all of their properties in sacks on their backs. On the hospital lawn in Sariwon, hundreds of patients were waiting for their hospitalization as the number of the beds was quite limited. At that time, the tuberculosis was widely spread across the country, 70-80 new patients came in daily while the total number of the beds in the pulmonology was only 50. Therefore, Dr. Böszörményi had to make a difficult decision about the patients' hospitalization: the patients with mild symptoms should receive medicines and be sent back to their home while the ones in critical condition, whose illness was far too advanced to save their lives, were also refused to be hospitalized. Only those patients in treatable conditions were accepted and taken care of. Dr. Böszörményi violated this rule once. A young woman in critical condition came to the hospital, where she was X-rayed. The woman was found no chances to be recovered, and she was sent to her home. However, in the evening of the same day when Dr. Böszörményi was examining new patients in front of the hospital, he identified the aforementioned young woman among the other waiting people. She was in critical condition, almost unconscious. She was with a few-month-old infant who was inseparable from the mother who was still alive. Of course, the baby needed someone to look after it. Dr. Böszörményi decided to accept both the mother and the infant to the hospital and the baby was

Dr. Miklós Böszörményi, Humngarian pulmonologist
(Semmelweis Medical History Museum, Budapest)

hospitalized in the pediatrics. After a few days, the woman passed away, but her child survived and was transfered safely to a local orphanage.[9)]

Dr. Miklós Böszörményi mentioned another fatal desease which occured in North Korea at that time. A type of bacteria caused coughing up blood and stroke. According to the local research of the Hungarian physicians, the bacteria was mainly found in a popular Korean food, *saeu-jeot*, salted raw shrimps. The Hungarians warned Korean people how dangerous the bacteria was, but it was hard to persuade them not to eat the raw shrimps. When a small boy died from the infection, his father asked the doctors to let him observe the kid's autopsy. The father said that he wanted to see the cause of his child's death with his own eyes and tell it to his villagers. However, the Hungarians did not allow him to observe

---

9) Letter written on November 1, 1986, by the Hungarian pulmonologist Dr. Miklós Böszörményi. HM HIM MN Kgy: C-305

A picture of Sariwon city, taken by a member of the sixth group of the Hungarian medical teams
(Semmelweis Medical History Museum, Budapest)

the autopsy.[10]

The Hungarian physicians experienced many times that the Koreans highly appreciated the medical knowledge of the Hungarians'. The Koreans always longed for medical information and knowledge, which was sympathized by the Hungarian doctors. For example, Dr. Miklós Böszörményi saw young Korean males standing and reading books for hours in the sole bookstore in Sariwon since they had not enough money to buy books. Sometimes their trust in books was too strong: the pulmonologist wrote that their Korean colleagues who had studied medicines with the old German medical textbooks were never willing to agree that the contents of the textbooks they studied with could be outdated. Dr. Böszörményi also mentioned the infantile aspect of Koreans at that time. In the early autumn of 1954, the local authorities planned to

---

10) "Koreában járt két ember..." (Two men from Korea – in Hungarian) *Új Hírnök*, August 30, 1997.

Dr. Frigyes Kulka with a Korean physician at the hospital in Hamheung. According to the memo on the backside of the photo, the Korean doctor wanted to be a lung surgeon.
(From the collection of Dr. Janina Kulka)

Dr. Frigyes Kulka with the staff of the first tuberculosis station in the DPRK
(From the collection of Dr. Janina Kulka)

set up a central heating system of the hospital in Sariwon. However, the only boiler which could be used for the system was already being used in the building of the local party commission. Therefore, the boiler was removed from the party building and transferred to the hospital. Installing the system was slow, but the Koreans reassured the physicians that the whole system should be ready by November 7, the anniversary of the 'Great October Socialist Revolution', the biggest holiday of the socialist countries. At the end of October, all the residents of Sariwon joined the voluntary work to finish the installation of the central heating and had it completed on November 7. The Koreans held a huge celebration on the occasion of the successful work. However, after a few days it became clear that the central heating did not work due to the misconnected pipes. It was very cold in the hospital during the winter as the Hungarians could provide only small radiators. One young patient in the pediatrics was frozen to death.[11)]

---

11) Letter written on November 1, 1986, by the Hungarian pulmonologist Dr.

Dr. Frigyes Kulka in Yongbyon in North Phyongan Province with a man named Park Chang-sik on January 24, 1956. On the backside of the photo was written a message in Korean: *'To my great benefactor, Respected Prof. Kulka. I will never forget it. My birthplace is: North Hamgyong Province, Kilju county, the 2nd part of Pongam village. Park Chang-sik'*
(From the collection of Dr. Janina Kulka)

Miklós Böszörményi. HM HIM MN Kgy: C-305

The physicians and nurses of the hospital in Yongbyon in North Phyongan Province. Dr. Frigyes Kulka is in the middle
(From the collection of Dr. Janina Kulka)

The farewell photo of the seventh group in Sariwon. The photo was taken on February 17, 1956
(From the collection of Dr. Janina Kulka)

László Gera, Hungarian X-ray technician
(Semmelweis Medical History Museum, Budapest)

Despite the aforementioned difficulties, the seventh group of the Hungarian medical teams found the hospital in good order when they arrived on March 10, 1955. Part of the total 40 members of the group had already served in North Korea with the previous groups. Dr. Frigyes Kulka, the aforementioned pulmonologist of the fifth group, explained in a radio interview that during his second term in North Korea, he had an opportunity to send the tuberculosis patients to the villages which had excellent surroundings for recovery. The Hungarian hospital in Sariwon had cooperated with three villages for the patients' recovery. In return, they assisted the establishment of the country's first-ever lung surgery hospital in Yongbyon. Dr. Kulka said in the interview that it was more than symbolic that the mountain next to the hospital in Yongbyon was called Yak-san which meant 'Medicine Mountain'. The local residents believed in the healing force of the mountain and also had a folk song about the mysterious Yak-san.[12)]

---

12) *A Jalu-folyótól a 38. szélességi fokig*, 7.

László Gera who was the X-ray technician in the fourth group again served for a new mission in the seventh group. According to the reminiscence written by Gera, the group travelled to North Korea on a plane, not by train the previous groups used. In Moscow, they were divided into two groups and flew on two small aircrafts. As Gera's plane arrived in Pyongyang first, from the garden of the Hungarian Embassy could he observe the landing of the second plane on the other side of the river. During his second term in Korea, Gera often visited the hospitals in the other provinces where Hungarian-made X-ray machines were in use. Once he flew on a very small aircraft which was able to accommodate only seven people who jammed onto a couple of benches instead of individual seats. The plane was used to carry paratroops during the war.[13)]

[13)] Letter written in November 1986, by the Hungarian X-ray technician László Gera. HM HIM MN Kgy: C-223

XIII. The influence of the revolution in 1956 and the handover of the hospital

The eighth and the last group of the Hungarian medical teams arrived in the DPRK on February 14, 1956. Mária Nagy, the operating room nurse who had served in the third group, took on a new mission and joined the last group. In her reminiscences, she emphasized the differences between her previous experience and the new observation: from Moscow to Pyongyang, the eighth group traveled by a comfortable sleeping car; and the hospital in Sariwon was 'almost like the European standard'. According to the nurse, she and her colleagues visited the former building of the Hungarian hospital in Mangyongdae which had been already used as a cadet school decorated with red carpets. They had received a permission to enter the building. Mária Nagy took the opportunity to leave the building through its back door to see the rear garden. She tried to look for their former shelters but they had already disappeared. The small Korean house where the female staff had been accommodated also disappeared. What she could see was only the rice fields where the village of Nam-ri used to be.[1)]

Some of the 33 members of the last group left significant cultural legacy. Dr. László Gyarmati, brother-in-law of the famous Hungarian poet Miklós Radnóti, took excellent artistic photos of everyday life in the country, which were handed down to the next

1) Letter written probably in 1986 by the Hungarian paramedic, Mária Nagy. HM HIM MN Kgy: C-223

The main building of the Hungarian hospital in Sariwon. The photo was taken in 1956
(From the heritage of Dr. Lajos Fazekas)

The quarters of the Hungarian physicians in Sariwon city
(From the heritage of Dr. Lajos Fazekas)

Dr. Lajos Fazekas in front of the aircraft of the Chosun Minyong Hangkong airline at the airport of Pyongyang in March 1956. According to the memo on the back side of the picture, the internist was departing to the city of Hamheung
(From the heritage of Dr. Lajos Fazekas)

The picture was taken in front of the hospital in Haeju in April 1956. The institution was supported by the Hungarian medical teams. The third person from the right is internist Dr. Lajos Fazekas.
(From the heritage of Dr. Lajos Fazekas)

The May Day rally in the city of Sariwon in 1956. The picture was taken by a member of the eighth group of the Hungarian medical teams
(From the collection of Fortepan)

generations. One of the group members, internist Dr. Lajos Fazekas, wrote 11 articles about his observations on Korea. The articles were published from April 1957 in the Hungarian local paper *Félegyházi Közlöny*. According to the detailed articles, although the population of Sariwon city decreased to 100,000 after the war, the Hungarian hospital tried to take care of all of the 1,5 million citizens in North Hwanghe Province. The institution had 400 beds for patients in different departments and provided surgical services. The hospital also had a school for paramedics and nurses. All departments were operated by Hungarian doctors with the assistance of the young Korean deputies who just finished their medical studies.[2)] According

Members of the eighth group with American MP guards in Panmunjom on September 4, 1956. The second person from the right side is Dr. János Szederkényi, director of the Hungarian hospital. The person on the very left is Dr. Lajos Fazekas
(From the heritage of Dr. Lajos Fazekas)

to Dr. Fazekas, the Hungarian doctors resided in a separate building located in the garden of the hospital. The building had a separate Hungarian kitchen and a Hungarian cook.[3] To 'survive' from the summer heat in Sariwon, the Hungarian doctors built a concrete swimming pool used by the medical staff day and night.

The articles of Dr. Lajos Fazekas also confirm that in the mid-1950s, the foreigners including the Hungarian physicians were relatively free to move around within North Korea. In September 1956, the Hungarian doctors made an excursion to Panmunjom and took some pictures with American soldiers, which is not allowed nowadays. The Hungarians also met a South Korean reporter who took dozens of pictures of the doctors. The doctors were surprised

---

2) Fazekas, Lajos: "Nincs titokzatos dolog Keleten. II. rész" (There are no secrets in the East – in Hungarian) *Félegyházi Közlöny*, April 21, 1957.

3) Fazekas, Lajos: "Nincs titokzatos dolog Keleten. II. rész" (There are no secrets in the East – in Hungarian) *Félegyházi Közlöny*, April 21, 1957.

The barracks in Panmunjom. The picture was taken by a member of the eighth group of the Hungarian medical teams
(From the collection of Fortepan)

as they did not know why he did so. The Czechoslovakian members of the Neutral Nations Supervisory Commission told them the South Korean reporter probably mistook Dr. János Szederkényi for someone else. The reporter might take so many pictures of him as he was a very good-looking, elegant gentleman with gray wavy hair and a brilliant goatee, which made him look like a great politician.[4)]

Even though it is not mentioned in Dr. Fazekas's contemporary articles, during the turbulent autumn of 1956, he was responsible for taking one of his colleagues back to Budapest. The Hungarian physician, Dr. Miklós Magyar, was suffering from the side effect of a medicine called chloramphenicol. Since he was in his critical condition, he had to be sent back to Budapest by plane urgently. However, they wasted too much time during the transit in Moscow and also, the revolutionary situation in Hungary did not allow

---

4) Fazekas, Lajos: "Nincs titokzatos dolog Keleten. II. rész" (There are no secrets in the East – in Hungarian) *Félegyházi Közlöny*, April 21, 1957.

Dr. Miklós Magyar, the only Hungarian citizen whose death was indirectly connected to his service in North Korea
(Semmelweis Medical History Museum, Budapest)

the plane to land in Budapest but in Prague. Finally, the patient passed away inside the airport of Prague.[5] According to the son of Dr. Fazekas, the corpse of the physician was transported to Hungary by the Soviet army. Dr. Miklós Magyar was the only Hungarian physician whose death was connected to his service in North Korea.[6]

From the autumn of 1956, the name of the former Hungarian party leader, Mátyás Rákosi, had been removed from the official name of the Hungarian hospital, which happend a few month after the replacement of Rákosi by the Soviets. However, the internal tensions in Hungary brought the revolution, and anti-Soviet freedom fights in Hungary started in October 23, 1956. According to the reminiscence written by the former Hungarian Ambassador to Pyongyang, Károly Práth, the most difficult time of his diplomatic service in North Korea was the autumn of 1956.[7] The physicians

---

5) *A magyar patológia története*. (History of the Hungarian pathology – in Hungarian) (Ed. Bodó, Miklós et al.) Budapest: Medicina, 2005, 248.

6) The author's conversation with Dr. Tamás Fazekas, son of the interist physician Dr. Lajos Fazekas. (Szeged, December 19, 2014.)

7) Letter written on November 26, 1986, by the former Hungarian Ambassador

heard about the outbreak of the revolution and its progress. Many of them received telegrams from their families describing the situation. A dermatologist doctor received a telegram saying that his family escaped from Hungary to abroad. The doctor also decided to escape from the Soviet bloc and defect to so-called 'free world'. It was obvious that the shortcut was to cross the 38th parallel. The aforementioned doctor tried to escape to South Korea, but he was caught by the North Korean authorities in Kaesong.[8)]

Károly Práth wrote in his diplomatic report that two other physicians, a radiologist and a pediatrician, also wanted to leave North Korea. On November 3, 1956, the two doctors suggested the others that they should have their passports back from the embassy and leave the country together. They wanted to join the International Red Cross in China. In the morning of November 5, the tension was mounting in the hospital because the pediatrician declared that he decided to leave the country. The radiologist said that for the first time in his life, he 'took control of his destiny'. To relieve the tension, Ambassador Károly Práth personally went to Sariwon at noon on the same day to give a speech to the physicians. He told them that the pro-Soviet government had been established in Hungary, which would create 'order' in the country soon. The words implies that the Ambassador, as an old communist cadre, fully supported the collaboration with the Soviets who repressed the revolutionary government of the Prime Minister Imre Nagy. The envoy asked the physicians to preserve the honour of the Hungarian medical teams which had been gained for many years in North Korea. Károly Práth had a separate talk with the dermatologist who decided not to leave the country after all while the radiologist and the pediatrician decided to leave. The 'collective of the physicians'

Dr. Károly Práth. HM HIM MN Kgy: C-305

8) Report written on November 14, 1956, by the Hungarian Ambassador Károly Práth. MNL XIX-J-1-j-1945-1964-Korea box no. 9. 13/g

The Hungarian Ambassador, Károly Práth is giving a speech during the inaguration of the bilingual monument in the garden of the Hungarian hospital. The photo was taken by Dr. László Gyarmati, brother-in-law of the famous Hungarian poet, Miklós Radnóti (Hungarian Military History Archive, MN Kgy: C-306/B)

stated that they no longer wanted to be in the same place with the two, so the Embassy bought the two doctors train tickets to Budapest and took measures for the doctors not to deviate from the assigned route.[9)]

On November 8, 1956, the the aforementioned director of the hospital, Dr. János Szederkényi, wrote a letter to the Ministry of Health in Budapest. He explained the reasons why the two physicians were sent back to Hungary. The director added one more reason of the return of the pediatrician; a verbal attack against a female employee in the hospital.[10)] However, according to the the

9) Report written on November 14, 1956, by the Hungarian Ambassador Károly Práth. MNL XIX-J-1-j-1945-1964-Korea box no. 9. 13/g

10) Letter written on November 8, 1956, by the hospital director Dr. János Szederkényi. MNL XIX-J-1-j-1945-1964-Korea box no. 9. 13/g

Ambassador Károly Práth and the last members of the Hungarian medical team in front of the bilingual monument in the garden of the Hungarian hospital
(Hungarian Military History Archive, MN Kgy: C-306/B)

Ambassador's report written on April 10, 1957, this issue had not come to an end yet. The two visited family members' of their former colleagues and told them about the turbulence in the Hungarian hospital that happend during the revolution. This made some wives consider their husbands as a 'traitor' of the revolution. In the mean time, the two doctors were nominated for the university professors in Hungary, which the physicians who remained in North Korea were not particularly happy about. Károly Práth illustrated the mood with the followings. They tried to establish the local unit of the [pro-Soviet] Hungarian Socialist Worker's Party. However, only three out of fourteen Hungarians spoke their mind to join the unit. The three were the director of the hospital, an operating theater assistant and the cook.[11)]

---

11) Report written on April 10, 1957, by the Hungarian Ambassador Károly Práth. MNL XIX-J-1-k-1945-1964-Korea box no. 9. 18/b

The author in his capacity as the Hungarian Ambassador accredited to the Republic of Korea and the DPRK in front of the bilingual monument in the People's Hospital of North Hwanghae Province in North Korea
(From the collection of the author)

30 years later, the former Ambassador Károly Práth stated in his reminiscence that the termination of the activities of the Hungarian medical teams in the DPRK was greatly influenced by the Hungarian revolution in 1956.[12)] Since the agreement on the handover of the hospital was signed in June 1957, the hospital had belonged to the Health Ministry of the DPRK. To commemorate the activities of the Hungarian physicians, a bilingual monument was erected in the garden of the hospital in Sariwon City.

12) Letter written on November 26, 1986, by the former Hungarian Ambassador Dr. Károly Práth. HM HIM MN Kgy: C-305

XIV. Aftermath of the Hungarian medical support

The members of the Hungarian medical teams who served in North Korea during and after the Korean War became important symbolic figures in the history of North Korean – Hungarian ties which had lasted until the collapse of the socialism in Central and Eastern Europe. The elderly physicians and nurses used to be invited to the annual receptions of the Embassy of the DPRK and some of them had opportunites to visit the country again. Dr. Ödön Sátori traveled to Pyongyang again twenty years after his return to Hungary as a team doctor of the Hungarian athletic group. The doctor had his North Korean state award pinned up on his suit during the reception which was held by the North Korean hosts. The North Koreans were pleasantly surprised at the award and offered him to stay at a luxury apartment instead of the reserved ordinary hotel room. In addition, a North Korean vice minister organized a special reception in honor of the Hungarian physician.[1)] Dr. János Bonta, the radiologist of the third medical group, also had an opportunity to visit the DPRK in the 1960s. However, it was impossible for him to meet any of his former North Korean colleagues. He said when he was escorted to Mangyongdae, the former hospital buildings were being used by the Mangyongdae Revolutionary School, which made the doctors banned to enter the buildings. Dr. Bonta also mentioned a trouble he had in the country when he carried a small

1) Sátori, *Koreai emlékeim II*, 3.

The North Korean propaganda photo about the former building of the Hungarian hospital in Mangyongdae. The building belonged to the Mangyongdae Revolutionary School (Hungarian Military History Archive, MN Kgy C-230)

opera binocular which was misunderstood by the North Koreans as a suspicous object. Also, a former North Korean nurse who got married to a Hungarian physician was able to see her Korean family in the DPRK only for an hour before her departure back to Hungary.[2)]

From the mid-1980s, the elderly physicians and nurses formed an informal association of which the nomial leader was Dr. Frigyes Kulka, one of the members of the fifth and the seventh

2) Bihari, Tamás: "Elfelejtett internacionalisták" (Forgotten internacionalists – in Hungarian) *A Világ*, January 11, 1990.

medical group. However, the actual leader was the aforementioned supplier Tibor Heltai, a member of the first and the second group.[3] In 1983, Heltai spent one month as a guest in the Hungarian Embassy in Pyongyang. In 1985, he organized a group travel for 47 former physicians and nurses to the 40th anniversary of the liberation of the Korean Peninsula from the Japanese colonial rule. According to his recollection, the group traveled to Pyongyang from Moscow by a huge Soviet-made Ilyushin passenger plane. The journey took less than 8 hours, which was a lot shorter compared to the journey in the 1950s as most of the Hungarian physicians travelled to North Korea on the Trans-Siberian railway, which took more than a week. The group spent 16 days in the DPRK, visited their 'former workplace' – probably in Sariwon – and climbed the Geumgang Mountain. According to the reminiscence, the elderly physicians were impressed by the development of the country. The capital, in particular, was in huge contrast with its former condition.[4]

Tibor Heltai played a significant role in the pioneering documentation on the Hungarian hospital in Korea. In the second half of the 1980s, he asked his former colleagues to write about their experiences in Korea, collected the manuscripts and kept them in the archives. He also asked the former envoys who served in the

---

3) According to an article about Tibor Heltai, his life was more than adventurous. In 1944, he joined the Soviet troops in Northern Hungary and led them behind the German lines. After the WW2, served as the party chief in the provincial city of Tata, became aircraft navigator at the Maszovlet airlines, was a responsible cadre for the nationalization of the private banks and in 1950, he was sent to North Korea as the supplier of the first and the second medical group. In 1956, during the anti-Soviet revolution in Hungary, he fought against the freedom fighters along with the Soviet troops. He also participated in the Vietnam War, as one of the Hungarian delegates to the International Control Commission in Saigon. In the 1980s, he was known as a very active member of various associations and often gave lectures about his experiences in North Korea and South Vietnam. Source: Rózsa, László: "A korszerűtlen ember" (The outdated man – in Hungarian) *Népszabadság*, October 7, 1986.

4) Letter written in November 1986, by the Hungarian X-ray technician László Gera. HM HIM MN Kgy: C-223

Károly Pásztor (the second from the right in the first row) at the Hungarian hospital in Mangyongdae. Kwon Oh-jik, a former North Korean envoy to Budapest is in the center of the first row, and Major Hwang Su-bong, deputy director of the Hungarian hospital is on the the right of the second row
(Photo Archive of the Hungarian Ministry of Defense, Budapest)

DPRK in 1950s for the same. Unfortunately, Sándor Simics, the first Hungarian envoy to North Korea passed away in 1978 but Károly Pásztor, a retired colonel who served in Pyongyang between 1951 and 1954 was still alive.[5] The retired gentleman was living in the provincial city of Miskolc at that time. Even though he was out of shape, he sent a handwritten letter to the former supplier. Pásztor wrote in his letter that after he was appointed as the Ambassador to North Korea, the party leader Mátyás Rákosi called him for a meeting and asked him why he wore his wedding ring. The newly appointed envoy immediately removed the ring from his finger while his wife who remained in Hungary became very sad. Pásztor

---

5) Pásztor, Károly (1913-?): Hungarian soldier and a communist cadre. He was born in Northern Hungary in a poor peasant family and worked in the iron complex of the industrial town of Diósgyőr. After the WWII, he became officer in the Hungarian People's Army. His only diplomatic service was in Pyongyang.

Hungarian Ambassador Károly Práth (on the left) in the Hungarian hospital in Sariwon
(Hungarian Military History Archive, MN Kgy: C-306/B)

recalled that his vehicle was often attacked by the aircrafts during his frequent trips to China; his first car, a Soviet-made Pobeda, was perforated by bullets. The retired colonel mentioned several other occasions when he had to jump out of the car to go and hide in a shelter. Once, he had to lie down flat on the muddy rice field in his newly made white suit and even lost one of his shoes in the marsh. He wrote about the terrible road condition in North Korea. The road surface was damaged by tire marks and it was always covered with dust. The aircrafts could easily detect the vehicles due to the dust cloud they made. The handwritten letter also mentioned that he really liked Korean people during his service, but he still did not know why he was suddenly recalled to Hungary by the Foreign Ministry before finishing his service. His sudden departure did not allow him enough time to say good bye to his Korean colleagues.[6)]

In 1958, one year after the last Hungarian group left, Ambassador Károly Práth presented Hungarian state awards to the staff of the hospital in Sariwon. The picture was taken after the awarding ceremony. The fifth person from right in the seated row is Han Sor-ya (1900-1976), a writer who was one of the most important cadres in the North Korean cultural affairs in the 1950s (National Archives of Hungary, Ministry of Foreign Affairs' Directory)

The reason of his recall was the same as his appointment: Pásztor was a professional soldier, an important manpower during the war, but the armistice required another types of cadre for the mission. This theory is supported by the the fact that with the arrival of the next envoy, the diplomatic relations between Hungary and North Korea was re-established on the ambassadorial level.

The next envoy, Ambassador Pál Szarvas who had served between 1954 and 1956 passed away in 1971. Therefore, when the aforementioned Tibor Heltai was collecting the reminiscences about the Hungarian hospital, he could reach only Ambassador Károly Práth who had served from 1956 to 1961.[7] In the long letter the

---

6) Letter written on November 6, 1986, by the former Hungarian envoy Károly Pásztor. HM HIM MN Kgy: C-305

7) Práth, Károly (1910-1994): Hungarian comunist worker and diplomat. From his young age, he actively participated in the communist movement and fought in the Spanish Civil War as the member of the International Brigades. In 1942, he was transported from Hungary to the Eastern Front to do labour service in the Hungarian Army. However, he defected to the Soviet troops in

elderly Ambassador wrote, he recalled that his wife had a high fever when they departed to the DPRK in early July 1956. The couple spent a day in Moscow where Práth had already visited in 1943 after completing his partisan training in the Soviet Red Army. At that time, all the houses were painted in sand color for camouflage. The Ambassador and his ill spouse reached Beijing via Novosibirsk by plane and continued their travel to North Korea by train. When they arrived in Pyongyang, the diplomat was shocked at the view of the collapsed station and the destroyed city. One and a half months after their arrival, the Ambassador's wife was transported to the Hungarian hospital in critical condition. According to the envoy's reminiscence, his wife suffered from dysentery which was not a serious desease in Hungary at that time. Unfortunately the hospital in Sariwon did not have any medicines to treat the disease. Práth visited her wife in the hospital every day while the director told him he had to prepare himself for the worst-case scenario. Eventually, she was provided with an effective Swiss-made medication and recovered after two weeks. As it was mentioned above, the most difficult period in his diplomatic service was when the Hungarian revolution started in the autumn of 1956, which casued the termination of the activities of the Hungarian medical teams in the DPRK.[8)]

In the late 1980s, some of the elderly physicians joined the Hungarian Partisan Federation. It was composed of the former Hungarian resistants who fought against the Nazis during the WWII. After the fall of the Communism in 1989, the organization changed its name to Hungarian Resistants and Antifascists

---

1943. He fought as a partisan in Western Ukraine and Northern Hungary along with the Soviet troops. In the early 1950s, he was a party official. Later, he served as the Hungarian Ambassador in Pyongyang between 1956 and 1961, and in Sofia between 1961 and 1963.

8) Letter written on November 26, 1986, by the former Hungarian Ambassador Dr. Károly Práth. HM HIM MN Kgy: C-305

High level Hungarian delegation arrives in Pyongyang in the late 1970s. Dr. Frigyes Kulka seems to be in the back, on the right from the rear part of the aircraft
(From the collection of Dr. Janina Kulka)

High level Hungarian delegation in Mangyongdae in front of the birthplace of Kim Il-sung in the late 1970s. Dr. Frigyes Kulka is the second from the left
(From the collection of Dr. Janina Kulka)

A recent photo of the People's Hospital of North Hwanghae Province in the DPRK. The slogan on the main gate is: 'Comrade Kim Il-sung and Comrade Kim Jong-il will be forever with us'
(From the collection of the author)

Association. It combined with a special group of the retired doctors who had served in Korea. It is worth noting that in the autumn of 1989 when the South Korean president Roh Tae-woo visited Hungary to expand the bilateral ties which was established earlier that year, the elderly physicians received unexpected English letters written by an alleged South Korean student, Kim Dal-hyun (probably a pseudonym). He warned the readers how dangerous it was to establish the diplomatic relations between Hungary and South Korea. All the elderly doctors who served in North Korea read the letters, but some of them were wondering how the alleged South Korean student knew their current postal address as it had been changed several times. It is assumed that the letters were most likely written by the North Korean propaganda machine with the assistance of the DPRK legation in Budapest.[9)]

---

9) Bihari, Tamás: "Elfelejtett internacionalisták" (Forgotten internacionalists –

After Dr. Frigyes Kulka, the nominal leader of the informal association passed away in the autumn of 1989, Tibor Heltai did his best to keep the association and organized a new meeting for the elderly physicians in early 1990. However, in the process of the regime change, new problems and challanges emerged from the Hungarian society, and the reputations of the former Hungarian medical teams in North Korea became faded away. The manuscripts and the documents collected by the physicians were planned to be transferred to the Zrínyi Military Publishing House who eventually did not accept them due to the lack of potential readers.[10] The last document in the archive file of the former medical teams is a condolence letter written by three elderlies addressed to the DPRK legation in Budapest on the occasion of Kim Il-sung's death in 1994.[11]

---

in Hungarian) *A Világ*, January 11, 1990.

10) Bihari, Tamás: "Elfelejtett internacionalisták" (Forgotten internacionalists – in Hungarian) *A Világ*, January 11, 1990.

11) Letter sent to the North Korean chargé d'affaires in Budapest. HM HIM MN Kgy: C-306

XV. The role of the medical teams in the intercultural exchanges

The Hungarian physicians and nurses in North Korea played a special role in the exchange of the culture between the two countries geographically far away from each other. The Hungarians learned a lot about the Korean culture while they served in North Korea. Some of the physicians published articles in the Hungarian newspapers not only about the local circumstances but also about the Korean culture. Koreans were also open-minded to accept the Hungarian culture. Some of them learned the Hungarian language quickly.

On March 15, 1951, the second group of the Hungarian medical teams hosted the Hungarian National Day event in Changchun to commemorate the anniversary of the Hungarian revolution and freedom fight of 1848. Military surgeon Dr. János Dénes mentioned in his reminiscences that at the event, the Korean deputy director of the hospital, Major Hwang Su-bong, recited the lyrics of the Korean translation of the Hungarian 'National song' written by the iconic Hungarian poet Sándor Petőfi.[1] According to

---

1) Petőfi, Sándor (1823-1849): Hungarian poet and revolutionary. He was born in the Southern plain of Hungary and started to write poems from his young age. He was interested in theatricals and joined to a travel theater. From 1844, his poems became more and more famous in Hungary. In 1848, he was the key person of the developments, who composed the iconic poem of the revolution called 'National song' ('Nemzeti dal' in Hungarian). He joined the Hungarian revolutionary army, but he killed in action during a battle with the Russian troops in Transylvania. The vast majority of his poems are compulsory curricula in Hungarian elementary and middle

The sight of a market in the DPRK in the mid 1950s. It is interesting to observe that the milieu on the looks more like the Chosun Kingdom than the Stalinist country. The photo was taken by Dr. László Gyarmati, brother-in-law of the famous Hungarian poet, Miklós Radnóti
(Hungarian Military History Archive, MN Kgy: C-306/B)

the surgeon, the poem seemed to be translated to Korean by Major Hwang himself.[2] In the spring of the following year, the famous Korean poet, Yim Hwa was hospitalized in the Hungarian hospital. The Hungarian diplomats and the leaders of the North Korean cultural community visited the hospital when the hospital hosted the May Day celebration. Yim Hwa told the Hungarians that he had read Petőfi's poems translated into Japanese and would like to translate the poems into Korean. Yim asked the diplomats to send him a book of Petőfi's poetry written in Russian.[3]

The famous composer Kim Soon-nam also participated in

schools.

2) Reminiscences of János Dénes, 15.

3) Report written on May 28, 1952, by the Hungarian envoy Károly Pásztor. MNL XIX-J-1-k-1945–1964-Korea box no. 9. 18/c.

A photo of vendors at the market, taken by Dr. László Gyarmati. It is interesting to observe that the traditional *hanbok* clothes were still worn every day at that time (Hungarian Military History Archive, MN Kgy: C-306/B)

the May Day event held in the hospital. He had planned for the bilateral cultural exchanges with Hungary. Kim who was the chairperson of the DPRK's Musicians Association at that time explained to the envoy that he learned of the two famous Hungarian composers, Béla Bartók (1881-1945) and Zoltán Kodály (1882-1967) when he was studying in Japan. Kim asked the envoy to send him sheet music of the two composers as well as that of the other contemporary Hungarian musicians. He was deeply attracted to the Hungarian folk songs, particularly to the 'revolutionary' ones. Kim also talked about his plans to promote the music of Bartók and Kodály under the umbrella of the DPRK's Musicians Association. According to the envoy's report, as they found these plans very beneficial to each other, they asked the ministry in Budapest to send sheet music and books about the Hungarian musicians written in Russian or German language together with LP records.4)

A photo of a traditional Korean medical office, taken by Dr. László Gyarmati
(Hungarian Military History Archive, MN Kgy: C-306/B)

However, both poet Yim Hwa and composer Kim Soon-nam were purged during the political campaign which targeted the cadres from South Korean. Consequently, their intercultural exchange plans were forgotten and they were portrayed as villains by the North Korean authorities. The Hungarian diplomatic report about the 3rd Congress of the Workers' Party of Korea which was held in April 1956 described Yim Hwa as a 'bourgeois reactionary' as he was the leader of the 'hostile writers'. Meanwhile, it was emphasized on the Congress that 'some of the North Korean artists' were fans of the Western European music since they did not pay enough attention to the Korean traditional music. It implied criticism of the purged composer Kim Soon-nam.[5)] It is interesting to add that in May 1952, envoy Pásztor Károly attached a photograph of the

4) Report written on May 28, 1952, by the Hungarian envoy Károly Pásztor. MNL XIX-J-1-k-1945–1964-Korea box no. 9. 18/c.

5) Report written on July 18, 1956, by the Hungarian chargé d'affaires Lajos Karsai. MNL XIX-J-1-k-1945-1964-Korea box no. 9. 18/d.

A photo of an elderly vendor who sells garlics and radishes, taken by Dr. László Gyarmati
(Hungarian Military History Archive, MN Kgy: C-306/B)

composer onto his report about the conversation shared with Kim Soon-nam. The photograph was discovered at the Hungarian National Archives by the author of this book, and its framed copy was handed over to Kim Se-won, the composer's daughter living in South Korea on November 3, 2020 at the Hungarian Embassy in Seoul.

In the field of the cultural exchanges, the Hungarians used a cine-projector to show Hungarian movies to the staff as well as to the patients. According to the report of Károly Pásztor, the screening in the hospital of Mangyongdae was held every Saturday. The following famous Hungarian movies were shown: the 'Talpalatnyi föld' ('Land of a human'); the 'Déryné' ('Mrs. Déry'); and the 'Ludas Matyi' ('Mattie the Goose-Boy').[6] According to the

6) Report written on June 11, 1952, by the Hungarian envoy Károly Pásztor. MNL XIX-J-1-k box no. 12. 28/c.

A photo of Korean kids, taken by Dr. László Gyarmati
(Hungarian Military History Archive, MN Kgy: C-306/B)

reminiscence of the technican László Gera, he held the movie screening for the patients several times in Mangyongdae and Huichon. The Hungarian actor, Kálmán Latabár (1902-1970) was particularly popular among the patients. The technican wrote that sometimes he hosted the movie screening on the mountains around Huichon using a stretched sheet to project to film on. The patients were able to watch the movie from both sides of the sheet.[7] After the armistice, Sariwon city became reconstructed well enough to build a movie theater which was first opened in 1955. According to the reminiscences of the Hungarian pulmonologist Dr. Miklós Böszörményi who served in the sixth group, the new theater screened a Hungarian film as well.[8] It was a propagandistic

---

7) Letter written in November 1986, by the Hungarian X-ray technician László Gera. HM HIM MN Kgy: C-223

8) "Koreában járt két ember…" (Two men from Korea – in Hungarian) *Új Hírnök*, August 30, 1997.

comedy, 'Állami Áruház' ('The State Department Store') which was made in 1952. The story is about a huge department store in Hungary operated during the early years of the socialist regime. The employees of the department store were divided into 'reactionaries' and the supporters of the new political system and battled each other. The pulmonologist mentioned that the North Koreans really liked the kissing scenes of the Hungarian movie as they could not find those intimate scenes in other movies which are still hard to find in the North Korean movies even after more than 60 years.

Regarding the movies, it should be mentioned that in October 1952, the possibility of shooting a documentary film about the Hungarian hospital was seriously discussed. In Pyongyang, János Papp, a Hungarian diplomat, wrote a report about the plan to make a documentary film as a co-production with North Korea and sent it to the Hungarian Ministry of Foreign Affairs. According to the report, the Hungarian diplomat suggested the idea of filming a documentary to a cadre at the DPRK's Ministry of Culture and Propaganda Affairs. The cadre answered that the documentary making is a North Korean task and 'obligation'. However, the Hungarian diplomat was opposed to the idea that North Korea solely made a movie, but suggested shooting it in co-production. The diplomat emphasized in his report that if the documentary was made by North Korea, it would include the activities of all the hospitals operated by the Central Eastern European countries in North Korea. The Hungarian hospital would be just one of many. However, in the case of a co-production, the Hungarian hospital will be in the main focus. The diplomat also emphasized in his report that the film-makers in North Korea had suffered from the technical difficulties and their film laboratory was operated in China where it was less easy to edit the film than in Budapest. János Papp also wrote that the only person who could write a scenario for the documentary was the aforementioned correspondent, Tibor Méray although the diplomat suggested the ministry find a Korean writer to write a scenario.[9]

Eventually, the political department at the Ministry of Foreign Affairs in Budapest canceled the plan to make the documentary. According to their 'diplomatic' answer, it was 'not nice' to focus mainly on the Hungarian hospital in a Hungarian - North Korean-made documentary when the other socialist countries were also operating hospitals in North Korea. The deputy head of the political department emphasized that if the 'Korean comrades' would like to shoot a movie on their own will and need some assistance, the Hungarian authorities were ready to give them what they would need. Moreover, the deputy head in Budapest wrote that it was a 'serious mistake' that János Papp, the diplomat at the Hungarian legation in Pyongyang, had talks with a cadre at the DPRK's Ministry of Culture and Propaganda Affairs about the plan of making a documentary film without any prior permission from Budapest.[10] Finally, the chargé d'affaires at the legation admitted with the ministry that they made a 'political mistake'.[11]

In the field of the cultural and personal contacts between the two far-away nations, it is necessary to emphasize that the first-ever Hungarian-Korean marriages were also observed at that time. In December 1954, Dr. Sándor Ditrói, the otolaryngologist physician informed the party secretary of the sixth group that he would like to marry Ri Yong-suk, the healthcare assistant of the hospital. The Korean woman was already pregnant with a child of the otolaryngologist. According to the report of the Hungarian party secretary, he forwarded the request directly to his North Korean

---

9) Report written on October 15, 1952, by diplomat János Papp. MNL XIX-J-1-k box no. 12. 28/c.

10) Letter written on November 18, 1952, by the deputy head of the political department Irén Rózsa. MNL XIX-J-1-k box no. 12. 28/c.

11) Report written on November 30, 1952, by chargé d'affaires Józsefné Turai. MNL XIX-J-1-k box no. 12. 28/c.

counterpart 'via the party line'. The chairperson of the party commission of North Hwanghae Province said that the marriage should be signed as soon as possible, but the final decision would be made by the government of the DPRK.[12] In February 1955, Dr. Ditrói again expressed his intention to get married to the North Korean woman to the DPRK's Ministry of Foreign Affairs. As the sixth group had to leave for Budapest in March, Dr. Ditrói asked Dr. Frigyes Kulka, the aforementioned pulmonologist of the seventh group, to speak for him in North Korea if neccessary.[13] In the meantime, the Hungarian party secretary tried his best to figure out what decision the North Korean government would make. Later, he learned that the North Korean side did not support the marriage. Géza Söjtöri, the party secretary, wrote in his report that the decision was not fair as he knew the Korean woman was a diligent and honest person. He also wrote that the Hungarian state had to help them get married.[14]

After returning to Hungary, Dr. Sándor Ditrói wrote a letter to the Hungarian Minister of Foreign Affairs to show his will to marry the Korean woman. He said that he was ready to travel back to North Korea at his own expense.[15] Meanwhile, the standpoint of the North Korean side seemd to be changed and the protocol chief of the DPRK Foreign Ministry initiated talks with the Hungarian Embassy in Pyongyang. On July 15, 1955, the cultural attache of the mission visited the ministry. The protocol chief tried to create a very negative image on the Korean women, but he said that North Korea would not oppose the 'release' of the woman if Hungary

---

12) Report written on August 1, 1955, by party secretary Géza Söjtöri. MNL XIX-J-1-k box no. 12. 28/c.

13) Letter written on July 26, 1955, by otolaryngologist Dr. Sándor Ditrói. MNL XIX-J-1-k box no. 12. 28/c.

14) Report written on August 1, 1955, by party secretary Géza Söjtöri. MNL XIX-J-1-k box no. 12. 28/c.

15) Letter written on July 26, 1955, by otolaryngologist Dr. Sándor Ditrói. MNL XIX-J-1-k box no. 12. 28/c.

Dr. Sándor Ditrói, the otolaryngologist physician and Ri Yong-suk, the healthcare assistant (second from right, with a headscarf) in the hospital in Sariwon
(From the collection of Éva Ditrói)

made an official request for it.[16)] After the Hungarian deputy Minister of Health Affairs talked about the marriage personally with Dr. Ditrói who again showed his intention to get married on September 1, 1955, the deputy minister asked the Hungarian diplomats to make efforts to solve the issue.[17)] On September 20, the regional department of the Hungarian Ministry of Foreign Affairs ordered the Embassy in Pyongyang to talk about the issue 'politely' with the North Koreans.[18)] The talk was obviously successful as the aforementioned deputy Minister of Health Affairs mentioned in his letter that two weeks later, the North Korean

---

16) Report written on July 16, 1955, by Ambassador Pál Szarvas. MNL XIX-J-1-k box no. 12. 28/c.

17) Letter written on September 1, 1955, by deputy minister Dr. István Simonovits. MNL XIX-J-1-k box no. 12. 28/c.

18) Order written on September 20, 1955, by the regional department of the Ministry of Foreign Affairs. MNL XIX-J-1-k box no. 12. 28/c.

authorities 'approved and supported' the marriage of the Hungarian physician and the Korean woman.[19] At the same time, a diplomat from the Hungarian Embassy in Pyongyang visited the consular department at the DPRK's Ministry of Foreign Affairs, where he was informed that the passport of the Korean woman was being issued. Also, the North Korean side expressed their regret that the marriage was 'delayed due to wrong information'.[20]

To sum up, the first-ever Hungarian-Korean international marriage was achieved successfully. It was not easy to collect the detailed information and reconstruct it from the available sources, but at least two other couples of Hungarian doctors – Korean women married at that time. Once, a high level Hungarian politician helped one of the couples to arrange the marriage according to the late diplomat, Dr. Károly Fendler who explained it to the author of this book. In the late 1950s, this issue ran into difficulties when North Korea was opposed to it. However, the physician who wanted to marry the North Korean woman was a card partner of the Hungarian Prime Minister, Dr. Ferenc Münnich. He asked for help to the Prime Minister to solve the issue. According to the words of the late diplomat, the Prime Minister did his best during his official visit to Pyongyang in May 1959. Dr. Ferenc Münnich told Kim Il-sung during the talks that the aforementioned Hungarian physician got seriously hurt 'in his heart' in North Korea.[21] Even though the high level political intervention was successful in this case, the North Korean leadership made all the possible efforts to be opposed to the international marriages from the early 1960s.

---

19) Letter written on October 6, 1955, by deputy minister Dr. István Simonovits. MNL XIX-J-1-k box no. 12. 28/c.

20) Report written on October 17, 1955, by chargé d'affaires József Füredi. MNL XIX-J-1-k box no. 12. 28/c.

21) The author's interview with Dr. Károly Fendler, who served at the Hungarian Embassy from the late 1950s. (Budapest, January 13, 2009.)

OVERVIEW

Hungarian medical teams in North Korea

Sequence of the Hungarian medical teams	Departure from Budapest	Arriving to the DPRK	Leaving from the DPRK	Location of the Hungarian medical teams	Arriving back to Budapest
1st group with 19 people	July 20, 1950	July 29, 1950	Oct. 27, 1950 to Manchuria March 12, 1951 from Changchun	**Chunghwa** Aug. 2, 1950 – Sept. 12, 1950 **Yangdok** Sept. 13, 1950 – Oct. 27, 1950 **Changchun** Dec. 5, 1950 – March 12, 1951	April 9, 1951
2nd group with 20 people	Febr. 11, 1951	Febr. 28, 1951 to Changchun June 26, 1951 to Mangyongdae	Jan. 27, 1952	**Changchun** Febr. 28, 1951 – June 23, 1951 **Mangyongdae** from June 26, 1951	Febr. 24, 1952
3rd group with 20 people	Dec. 28, 1951	Jan. 18, 1952	Oct. 2, 1952	**Mangyongdae**	Oct. 31, 1952
4st group with 24 people	Sept. 7, 1952	Sept. 26, 1952	June 26, 1953	**Mangyongdae** **Huichon** from March 1953	July 26, 1953
5th group with 25 people	June 1, 1953	June 19, 1953	March 22, 1954	**Huichon** **Songrim** from Nov 1953	April 18, 1954
6th group with 45 people	Febr. 19, 1954	March 14, 1954	March 25, 1955	**Songrim** **Sariwon** from May 1954	April 9, 1955
7th group 40 people	Febr. 24, 1955	March 10, 1955	Febr. 26, 1956	**Sariwon**	March 18, 1956
8th group with 33 people	Jan. 30, 1956	Febr. 14, 1956	Febr. 27, 1957	**Sariwon**	March 13, 1957

SOURCES

Published books and articles

Ahn, Dong-chun: *50nyon yeoreum.* (Summer '50 – in Korean) Pyongyang: Munhwa Yaesul Jonghap Chulphansa, 2001.

Baráthosi, Balogh Benedek: *Korea, a hajnalpír országa.* (Korea, land of the morning calm – in Hungarian) Budapest: A szerző kiadása, 1929.

Bozóky, Dezső: *Két év Keletázsiában. China és Korea.* (Two years in East Asia. China and Korea – in Hungarian) Nagyvárad: A szerző kiadása, 1911.

Faludi, Péter (real name: Fendler, Károly): *Mit kell tudni a Koreai Népi Demokratikus Köztársaságról?* (What should be known about the DPRK? – in Hungarian) Budapest: Kossuth Könyvkiadó, 1981.

Főkonzulok, követek és nagykövetek 1945-1990. (Consul generals, envoys and ambassadors 1945-1990 – in Hungarian) (Ed. Baráth, Magdolna – Gecsényi, Lajos) Budapest: MTA Bölcsészettudományi Kutatóközpont, 2015.

Gáspár, Ferenc: *Vitorlával Ázsia körül.* (With sails around Asia – in Hungarian) Budapest: Singer és Wolfner, 1907.

Mezey, István: *Az igazi Japán.* (The real Japan – in Hungarian) Budapest: Magyar Nippon-Társaság Kiadása, 1939.

Méray, Tibor: *Egy és más.* (Odds and Ends – in Hungarian) Budapest: Jószöveg Műhely Kiadó, 2012.

Méray, Tibor: *Koreai jelentés.* (Report on Korea – in Hungarian) Budapest: Szikra, 1953.

Méray, Tibor: *Tanuságtétel. Riportok a harcoló Koreáról.* (Testimony. Reports on Korea at war – in Hungarian) Budapest: Szikra, 1952.

Park Song-sun, "Hanguk tongripundongkwa Honggari," (The Korean independence movement and Hungary – in Korean) *Hangukkwa Honggari tongripundongui kiokkwa kyocha.* (The memories of the Korean and the Hungarian independence movements – in Korean) Jukjeon: Dankook University, 2019.

Szol, Csang Szik: *A barátság hőskölteménye.* (The Epos of Friendship – in

Hungarian) Budapest: Szépirodalmi Könyvkiadó, 1952.

Zoltán, János: *Add vissza az arcomat. Egy plasztikai sebész a koreai háborúban.* (Give back my face! A Plastic Surgeon in the Korean War – in Hungarian) Pusztazámor: DNM, 1996.

Archive of the Semmelweis Medical History Museum
(Hungary, Budapest)

Reminiscences of János Dénes (1943–1950–1958). Prepared by Tibor Heltai.

Diary of Ottó Diner (June 20, 1950 – July 19, 1951).

Diary of Antal Nádasi (September 26, 1952 – June 26, 1953).

Diary of Mihály Mincsev (January 1, 1953 – December 31, 1953).

Diary of József Balogh (June 1, 1953 – April 18, 1954).

Sátori, Ödön: *Koreai emlékeim I.* (My Korean memories 1 – manuscipt in Hungarian)

Sátori, Ödön: *Koreai emlékeim II.* (My Korean memories 2 – manuscipt in Hungarian)

Karády, Györgyné: *Magyar sebész orvos-egészségügyiek első koreai csoportjának menekülése az amerikai hadsereg elől Kínába.* (The escape of the first Hungarian medical team to China frontwards the American troops – manuscript in Hungarian)

National Archives of Hungary, Ministry of Foreign Affairs' Directory
(Hungary, Budapest)

MNL XIX-J-14 box no. 1.

MNL XIX-J-1-j-1945-1964-Korea box no. 9.

MNL XIX-J-1-k-1945–1964-Korea box no. 5.

MNL XIX-J-1-k-1945–1964-Korea box no. 9.

MNL XIX-J-1-k box no. 12.

Hungarian Ministry of Defense, Military History Archive
(Hungary, Budapest)

MN Kgy C-223
MN Kgy C-226
MN Kgy C-230
MN Kgy: C-290
MN Kgy: C-294
MN Kgy: C-305
MN Kgy: C-306
MN Kgy: C-306/B

Institute of Political History (Hungary, Budapest)

Tálas, Barna: *Egy Kína-kutató magyar diplomata emlékei a XX. század második feléből.* (Reminiscences of a Hungarian sinologist diplomat from the second half of the 20th century – manuscript in Hungarian)

Other document from private collection

A Jalu-folyótól a 38. szélességi fokig. (From the Yalu River to the 38th parallel – Text of a radio interview with Dr. Frigyes Kulka, written in 1956) Property of Dr. Janina Kulka

The author's interviews and conversitions with individuals

The author's interview with Dr. Károly Fendler, who served at the Hungarian Embassy from the late 1950s. (Budapest, January 13, 2009.)

The author's interview with Tibor Méray, who served as the Hungarian correspondent in North Korea during the Korean War. (Paris, December 16, 2012.)

The author's conversation with Dr. Tamás Fazekas, son of the interist physician Dr. Lajos Fazekas. (Szeged, December 19, 2014.)

The author's conversation with Éva Ditrói, daughter of nurse Ri Yong-

sook. (Budapest, February 26, 2019.)
The author's conversation with Dr. Ri Seong-chul, director of the People's Hospital of North Hwanghae Province in North Korea. (Sariwon city, April 3, 2019.)

APPENDIX

I. The evacuation route of the Hungarian physicians in October 1950.

Meanwhile, the diplomats of the Hungarian legation in Pyongyang were evacuated to the neighborhood of Shinuiju together with the whole diplomatic corps and crossed the Amnok (Yalu) River on November 2, 1950. The Hungarian diplomats wandered in Manchuria for five days and went back to North Korean territory via the town of Jian. Since then, the Hungarian legation had been operated at the border of Manpho until June 1951.

(Digital map design: J.C.)

II. The location of the Hungarian hospitals in the DPRK from the summer of 1951 until the spring of 1957.

Due to the bombardment onto the hospital in Mangyongdae, the institution moved to the mountainous region of Huichon in March 1953. After the armistice, the hospital was transfered to Songrim in October 1953. Finally, in 1954, the institution moved to the city of Sariwon.

(Digital map design: J.C.)

III. An article about the arrival of the Hungarian physicians was published in the *Rodong Shinmun* on August 3, 1950.

1950년8월3일 [목요일] 로동신문 [제215호]

조선근로자들은단결하라!

로동신문

사설

조선인민에게 주는 웽그리아인민의지성

김일성장군께

八월二일 아침보도

The following is the summary of the propagandistic article:

Hungarian people's devotion to the Korean nation

Our struggle is supported by the whole world. Hungary sent a medical team to Pyongyang to treat the wounded soldiers of the People's Army. The arrival of the Hungarian medical team is a proof of love for faith and peace. After Hungary was liberated from the Nazi repression by the armed force of the Soviet Union, the country moved towards socialism under the leadership of comrade Mátyás Rákosi and became a strong member of the peaceful nations. Thanks to Hungary for showing what the real friendship is during the time of the sadness, we warmly welcome the Hungarian physicians. We will reciprocate their efforts with our glorious victories.

(Source: MNL XIX-J-1-j-1945-1964-Korea box no. 9.)

IV. A special article with a group photo about the arrival of the Hungarian physicians was published in the *Rodong Shinmun* on August 3, 1950.

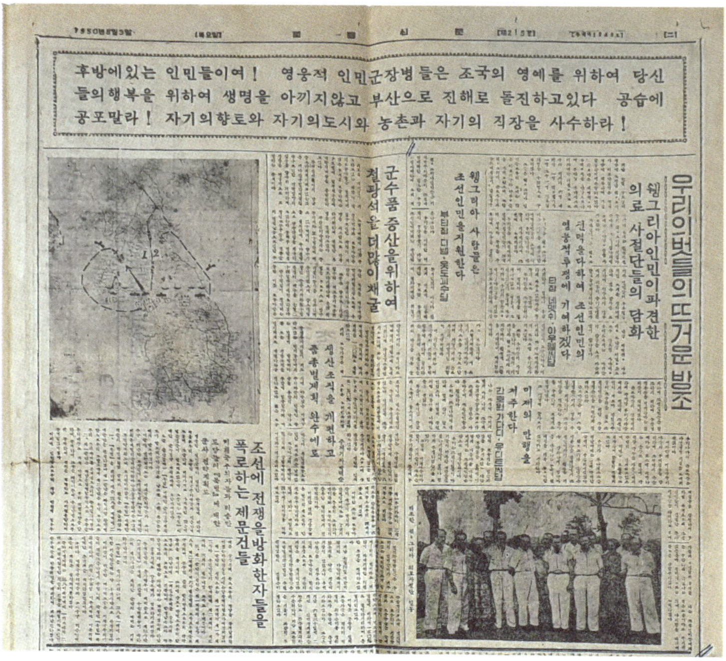

The headlines of the article are the followings:

Our friends are collaborating closely.
The physicians from Hungary gave speeches
'I will do my best to support the struggles of the Korean nation', said the political leader, Aurél Nemes.
'The Hungarians support the Korean nation!' told by the group leader, Dr. Ottó Diner

(Source: MNL XIX-J-1-j-1945-1964-Korea box no. 9.)

V. A radiotelegram from Budapest was sent to Dr. András László. The message was probably sent by his family member.

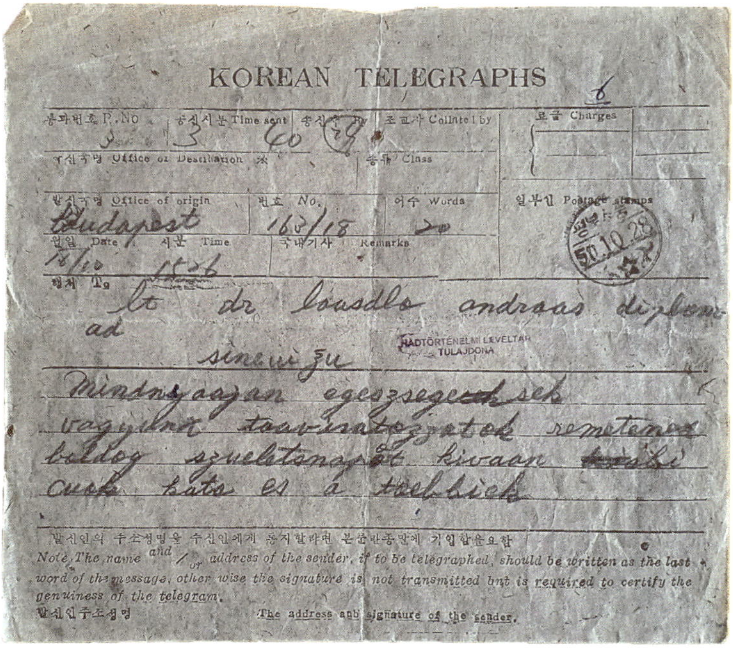
KOREAN TELEGRAPHS

P. No | Time sent | Collated by | Charges

Office of Destination | Class

Office of origin: Budapest | No.: 163/18 | Words: 20 | Postage stamps

Date: 18/10 | Time | Remarks

To: lt dr laaszlo andraas diplomad
sineuiju

Mindnyaajan egeszsegesek
vagyunk taaviratozzatok remeteknek
boldog szueletesnapot kivaan
cuca kato es a toebbiek

HADTÖRTÉNELMI LEVÉLTÁR TULAJDONA

Note, The name and/or address of the sender, if to be telegraphed, should be written as the last word of the message, other wise the signature is not transmitted bnt is required to certify the genuiness of the telegram.

The address and signature of the sender.

The telegram was delivered by the North Korean post on October 28, 1950 when the Hungarian medical team was already in the territory of Manchuria.

(Source: MN Kgy: C-306/B)

VI. The department of military health at the Headquarter of the Korean People's Army gave an award to Dr. Tibor Remete on February 1, 1951.

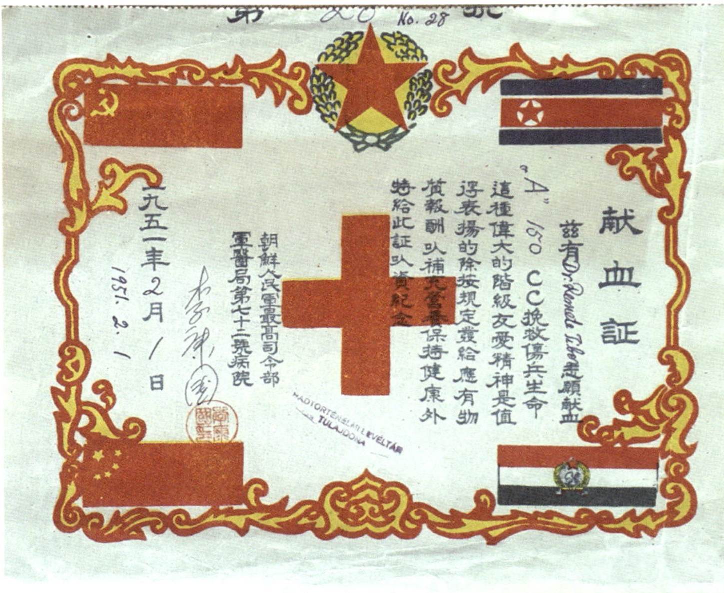

According to the document, Dr. Remete, the party secretary of the Hungarian medical team, donated blood and saved the life of a wounded soldier

(Source: MN Kgy: C-306/B)

VII. An invitation for the Hungarian National Day reception which was held to commemorate the '2nd anniversary of the constitution'.

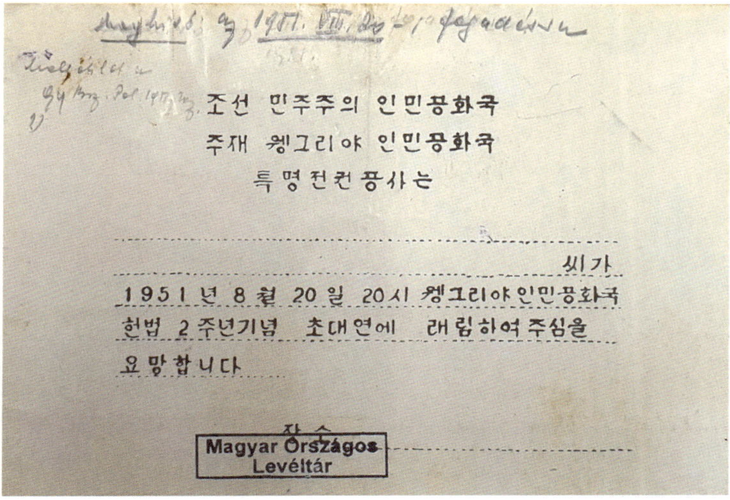
조선 민주주의 인민공화국
주재 웽그리아 인민공화국
특명전권공사는

씨가
1951 년 8 월 20 일 20시 웽그리아인민공화국
헌법 2주년기념 초대연에 래림하여 주심을
요망합니다

장소

The event started at 8 p.m. on August 20, 1951. The venue was the underground theater on the Moranbong Hill in Pyongyang

(MNL XIX-J-1-k-1945–1964-Korea box no. 5. 5/f)

VIII. 'The Epos of Friendship' written by Seol Chung-sik was dedicated to the Hungarian doctors during his two-month-long recovery in the hospital.

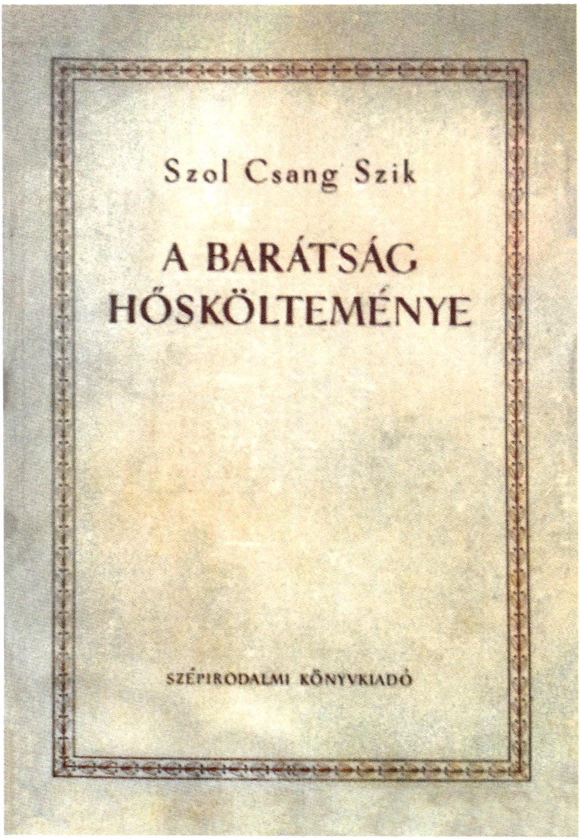

The poem was published in Budapest in 1952. One copy was sent to the poet in North Korea in January 1953. However, the Hungarian daily *Szabad Nép* reported in August 1953 that the poet was sentenced to death and executed.

(Source: From the collection of the author)

IX-X. A letter written in Hungarian language by Major Hwang Su-bong for the leader of the fourth Hungarian group.

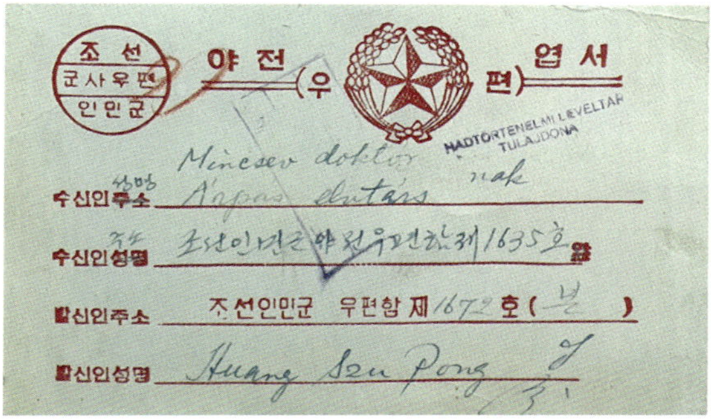
조선 군사우편 인민군

야전 (우 편) 엽서

수신인주소 상병 Mincsev doktor nak Árpás elvtárs

수신인성명 주소 조선인민군 야전우편함 제1635호

발신인주소 조선인민군 우편함 제1672호(본)

발신인성명 Huang Szu Pong

HADTÖRTÉNELMI LEVÉLTÁR TULAJDONA

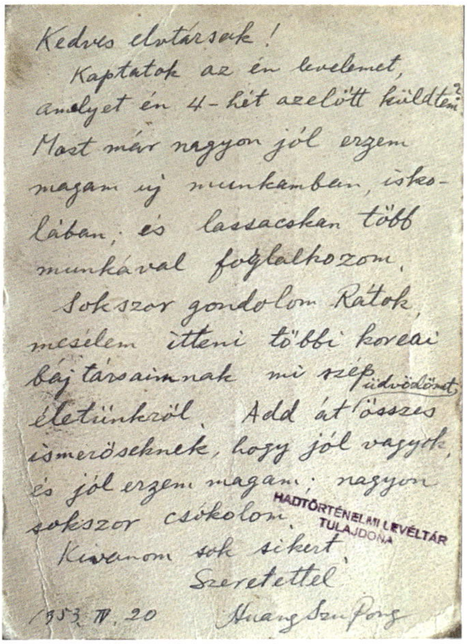
Kedves elvtársak!

Kaptatok az én levelemet, amelyet én 4-hét azelőtt küldtem?

Most már nagyon jól érzem magam új munkamban, iskolában, és lassacskan több munkával foglalkozom.

Sokszor gondolom Rátok, mesélem itteni többi koreai baj társaimnak mi szép életünkről. Add át üdvözlöst összes ismerősöknek, hogy jól vagyok, és jól érzem magam; nagyon sokszor csókolom. Kívánom sok sikert,

Szeretettel

1953. IV. 20 Huang Szu Pong

HADTÖRTÉNELMI LEVÉLTÁR TULAJDONA

The letter was written in April 1953. Major Hwang had been the vice director of the Hungarian hospital since the establishment. According to the Hungarian reminiscences, he was well-educated and good at multiple languages. However, he was purged during the internal turbulences of the regime.

(Source: MN Kgy: C-306/B)

XI-XII. 'The Gentle hand' written by Yang Bok-yun was dedicated to the Hungarian physicians.

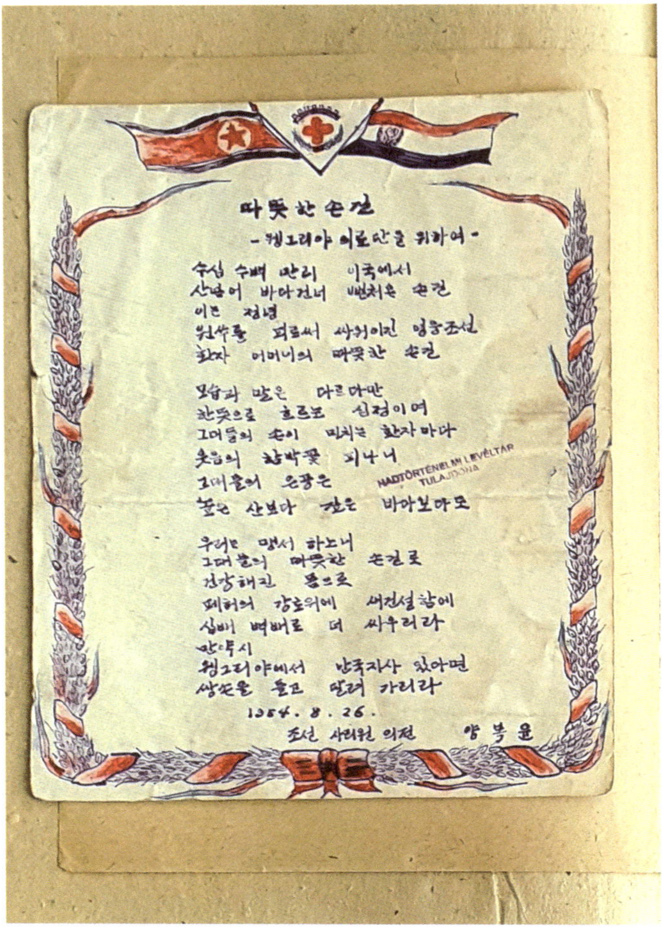

따뜻한 손길

- 웽그리아 의료단을 위하여 -

수십 수백 만리 이국에서
산넘어 바다건너 뻗치운 손길
이는 정녕
원쑤를 피로써 싸워이긴 영웅조선
환자 어머니의 따뜻한 손길

모습과 말은 다르다만
한뜻으로 흐르는 심정이여
그대들의 손이 미치는 환자마다
웃음의 함박꽃 피나니
그대들의 은공은
높은 산보다 깊은 바다보다도

우리는 맹서 하노니
그대들의 따뜻한 손길로
건강해진 몸으로
페허의 강토위에 새건설 함에
십배 백배로 더 싸우리라
만약시
웽그리아에서 난국지사 있아면
쌍손을 들고 달려 가리라

1954. 8. 26.

조선 사리원 의전 양복윤

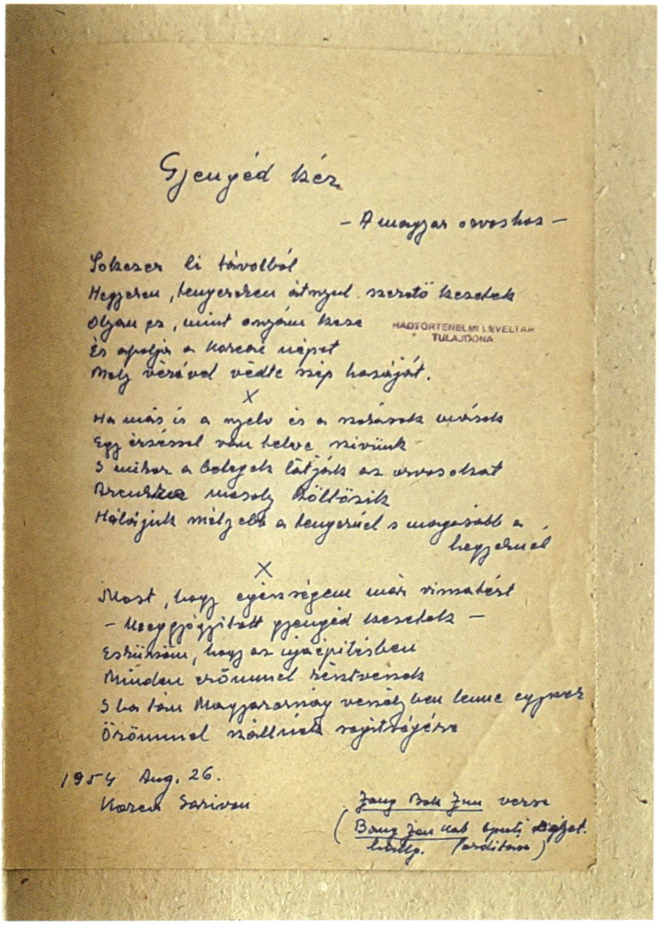

Gyengéd kéz

– A magyar orvoshoz –

Sokszor [illegible] távolból
Hegyeken, tengereken átnyúl szerető kezetek
Olyan az, mint anyám keze
És ápolja a koreai népet
Mely vérével védte szép hazáját.

X

Ha más is a nyelv és a szokások [illegible]
Egy érzéssel van telve szívünk
S mikor a betegek látják az orvosokat
Arcukra mosoly költözik
Hálájuk mélyebb a tengernél s magasabb a hegyeknél

X

Most, hogy egészségem már visszatért
– meggyógyították gyengéd kezeitek –
Esküszöm, hogy az újjáépítésben
Minden erőmmel résztveszek
S ha tán Magyarország [illegible] lenne egyszer
Örömmel szállnék [illegible]

1954 Aug. 26.
Korea Sariwon

Jang Bok Jun verse
(Bang Jon Kab egyet. hallg. fordítása)

The poem was translated into Hungarian by Bang Yong-gap, a university student who later became a North Korean diplomat, served in Budapest and played an important role in building the bilateral ties

(Source: MN Kgy: C-306/B)

XIII. An article about the departure of the sixth group to Budapest.

(3) (수요일) 황 북 일 보 第63호 (누계제1153호)

빛나는 업적을 남기고 귀국하는 웽그리야 의료단원들

사지과 의사 씨크야 노쉬 선생의 업적

환자에게 친절한 베네데크 임레 선생

The article was published in the *Hwangbuk Ilbo* on March 16, 1955. The following is the summary of the article.

The Hungarian medical team goes back home with brilliant results

The sixth group of the Hungarian medical teams arrived in our fatherland on March 2, 1954. The Hungarian group brought excellent medical technology and gentle internationalistic ideology. They were warmly welcomed by the people who got injured during the war and those who were suffering from incurable deseases. The Hungarian physicians remained in the main city of our province and gave material and technological assistance to reconstruct the medical infrastructure which had been destroyed by the war. Last year, they performed several difficult surgeries and achieved significat results in all the departments of the hospital. Because of the devoted work of the Hungarian physicians, many people could continue their happy lives. In the operating theaters, the leader of the group taught the Korean doctors a lot of new information kindheartedly. The Hungarians trained staff successfully: they gave the Korean paramedic students opportunities to learn from practices. They also gave opportunities of laboratory practices to all the staff of the medical institutions in the province. The people expressed their gratitude to the sixth group who achieved brilliant results.

(Source: Semmelweis Medical History Museum, Budapest)

XIV. An article about Dr. Frigyes Kulka, pulmonologist.

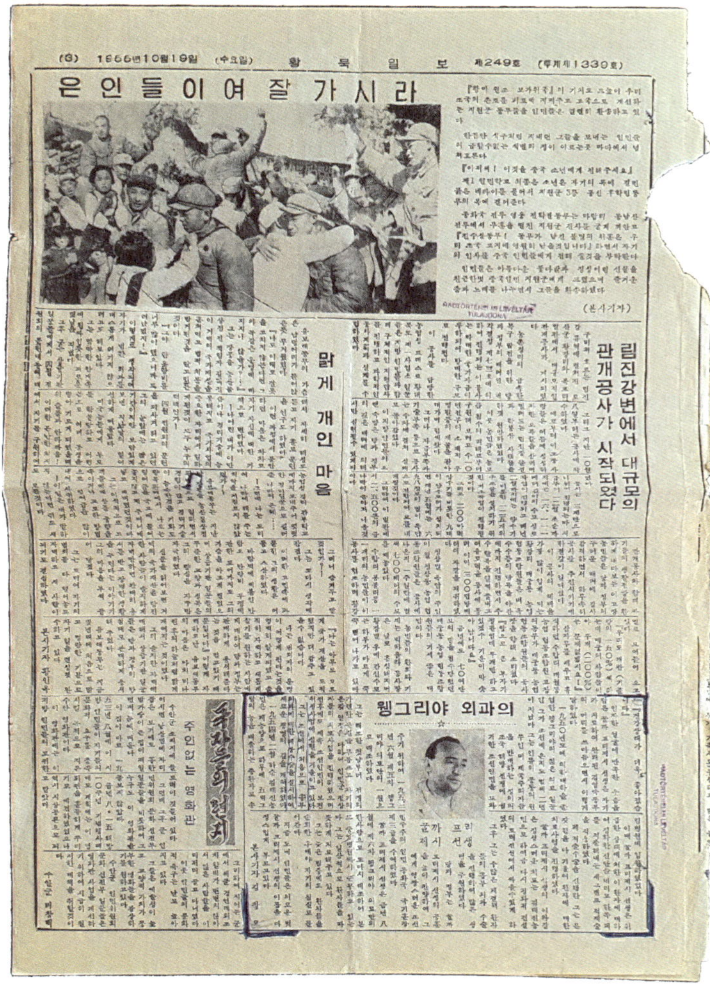

(3) 1955년10월19일 (수요일) 황 북 일 보 제249호 (루계제1339호)

은인들이여 잘 가시라

림진강변에서 대규모의 관개공사가 시작되였다

맑게 개인 마음

웽그리야 외과의

꿀까 프리제시 선생

주인없는 영화관

The article was published in the *Hwangbuk Ilbo* on October 19, 1955. The following is the summary of the article.

The Hungarian surgeon

Dr. Frigyes Kulka arrived in [North] *Korea in June 1953 as a member of the fifth Hungarian group. Upon arrival, the doctor started to treat the injured. After the war, he made efforts to improve the health and the physical conditions of the Korean people. He gave new lives to several people when he perfromed lung surgery on them and he made the first chest surgeries in our country. He saved lives of several people who had suffered from tuberculosis. In recognition of his services, the Party and the Government gave him the 3rd class of the National Flag award. In August, Dr. Kulka came again to* [North] *Korea as a member of the new Hungarian team and many people welcomed him warmly.*

(Source: MN Kgy: C-306/B)

XV. A 'Letter of Appreciation' issued by the health minister, Yi Byeong-nam, for Dr. Lajos Fazekas, internist, on February 20, 1957.

감 사 장

제8차 웽그리야 의료단

성 명 파제까쉬 라요쉬

이 동지는 조선민주주의인민공화국 전후 인민경제 복구발전 3개년 계획실행 기간에 인민보건 사업의 강화발전과 조선 웽그리야 량국 인민들간의 국제적 친선 단결을 도모함에 있어서 공적이 컸으므로 이에 감사를 드림

조선민주주의 인민공화국 내각

보건상 리병남

1957년 2 월 20 일

평 양

All the Hungarian physicians and staff members who served in North Korea received similar Letters of Appreciation and North Korean state awards.

(Source: From the heritage of Dr. Lajos Fazekas)

XVI-XVII. **A letter written and sent by Jin Yeon-ok, a North Korean nurse, to Irma Tóth, a Hungarian nurse.**

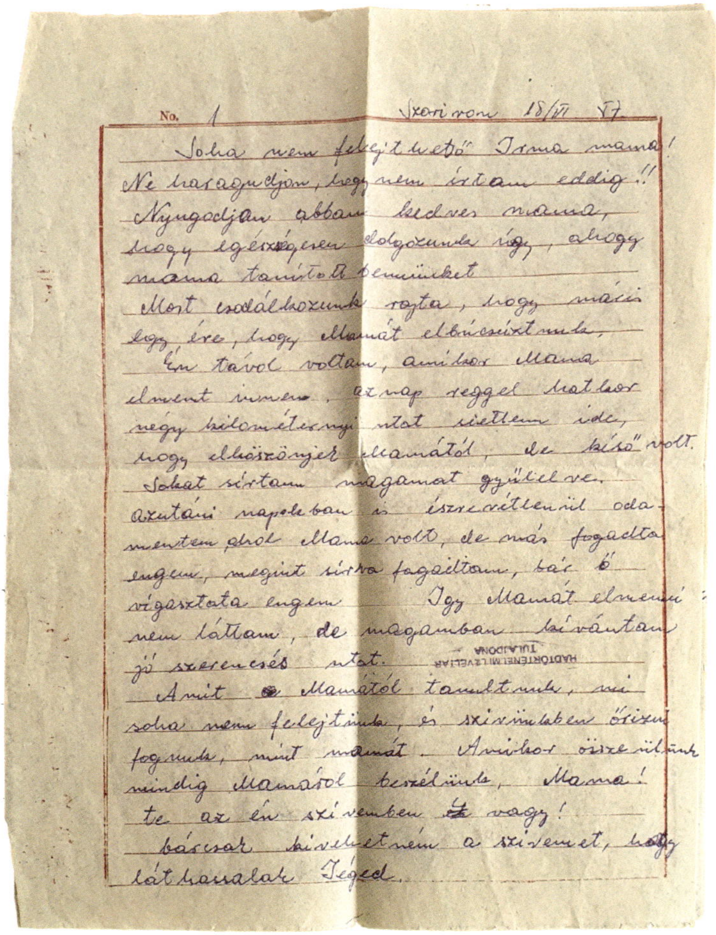

No. 1 Szariwon 18/VI 57.

Soha nem felejthető Irma mama!
Ne haragudjon, hogy nem írtam eddig!!
Nyugodjon abban kedves mama,
hogy egészségesen dolgozunk úgy, ahogy
mama tanította bennünket
Most csodálkozunk rajta, hogy máris
egy éve, hogy Mamát elbúcsúztunk.
Én távol voltam, amikor Mama
elment innen, aznap reggel hat kor
négy kilométernyi utat siettem ide,
hogy elbúcsúzzak Mamától, de késő volt.
Sokat sírtam magamat gyűlölve.
azutáni napokban is észrevétlenül oda-
mentem ahol Mama volt, de más fogadta
engem, megint sírva fogadtam, bár ő
vigasztalta engem. Igy Mamát elmenni
nem láttam, de magamban kívántam
jó szerencsés utat.

Amit a Mamától tanultunk, mi
soha nem felejtünk, és szívünkben őrizni
fogunk, mint mamát. Amikor összeülünk
mindig Mamáról beszélünk, Mama!
te az én szívemben vagy!
Bárcsak kivehetném a szívemet, hogy
láthassalak Téged.

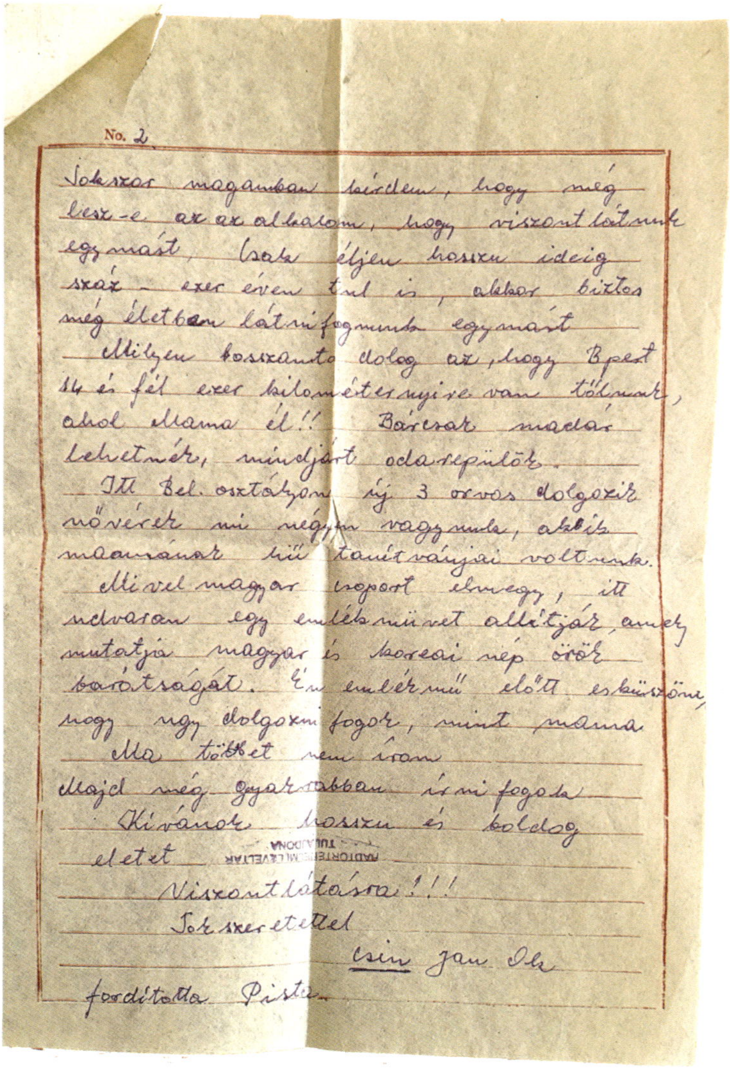
No. 2

Sokszor magamban kérdem, hogy még
lesz-e az az alkalom, hogy viszontlátnunk
egymást, csak éljen hosszu ideig
száz - ezer éven túl is, akkor biztos
még életben látni fogmunk egymást
Milyen hosszanto dolog az, hogy Bpest
14 és fél ezer kilométernyire van tőlünk,
ahol Mama él!! Bárcsak madár
lehetnék, mindjárt odarepülök.
Itt Bel. osztályon új 3 orvos dolgozik
nővérek mi négyen vagyunk, akik
mamanának kü tanítványai voltunk.
Mivel magyar csoport elment, itt
udvaran egy emlékművet állítják, amely
mutatja magyar és koreai nép örök
barátságát. Én emlékmű előtt esküszöm,
hogy úgy dolgozni fogok, mint mama.
Ma többet nem írom
Majd még gyakrabban írni fogok
Kívánok hosszu és boldog
életet
Viszontlátásra!!!
Sok szeretettel
Csin Jan Ok
fordította Piste.

The Hungarian woman served as a member of the seventh group in North Korea. The letter was written on June 18, 1957, more than one year after she went back to Budapest. During the activities of the Hungarian medical teams in North Korea, several close personal contacts were observed. These contacts ended immediately when the groups went back to Budapest.

This letter is a very good example of those personal contacts. The original copy of the letter was written in Korean and it was translated into Hungarian by a Korean boy who probably had studied in Budapest.

(Source: MN Kgy: C-306/B)

The translation of the letter written by Jin Yeon-ok:

Sariwon, June 18, 1957

To Mother Irma, the one I cannot forget.

Please don't be angry that I haven't written. Don't worry about us. Dear Mother, we are working healthily as Mother had taught us. It is hard to believe that it's been already a year since we said goodbye to you. I was far away [from the hospital] when Mother left and I walked four kilometers at 6 a.m. in that morning to say goodbye to Mother. However, I was too late. I cried a lot and I hated myself.

For the following days, I visited the workplace of Mother in secret and found another person working there, so I started to cry again. The new person tried to console me. I couldn't see Mother leaving but I just wished you a good journey in my mind.

We will never forget what we learned from Mother and keep all we had learned in our heart. We will also keep you in our heart, Mother! When we talk with each other, we always talk about you, Mother! Mother! You are in my heart! I wish I could take my heart out and see You in it!

I asked myself several times; will there be any chances to see each other again while we live? Please live a very long life, more than hundred years, more than thousand years. If so, we will see each other again for sure. How annoying it is that Budapest, where Mother is living, is 14 500 kilometers away from here! I wish I were a bird so I could fly there immediately!

Here in the Department of Internal Medicine are three new physicians working. We, the nurses, are four faithful pupils of you, Mother! Because the Hungarian medical team is leaving, a monument is being built in the garden to show the eternal friendship between the Hungarian and the Korean nation. Now, I promise myself in front of the monument that I will work like you, Mother!

I won't write more today, but I will write to you frequently. Wish you a long happy life! Good bye!

With full of love,

Jin Yeon-ok

XVIII. Hungarian and Korean nurses right before seventh group left for Budapest from the DPRK.

The second from the left is Irma Tóth, and one of the four Korean girls is probably Jin Yeon-ok

(Source: MN Kgy: C-306/B)

북한의 헝가리 의사들

부다페스트에서 한국전쟁으로!

2021년 6월 30일 1판 1쇄

지자 | Dr. Mózes Csoma
발행인 | 임종규
발행처 | (주)집문당
등록 | 1971. 3. 23. 제2012-000069호
주소 | 03134 서울시 종로구 돈화문로 32, 5층
전화 | +82-1811-7567
이메일 | sale@jipmoon.com
홈페이지 | www.jipmoon.com

ISBN 978-89-303-1909-6 93900

가격 35,000원